THE EARLY ARCHITECTURE OF
CHARLESTON

ACKNOWLEDGMENTS

THE EDITORS ACKNOWLEDGE THEIR GRATE-
FUL APPRECIATION OF THE KIND PERMISSION
OF THE ARCHITECTURAL FORUM AND J. B.
LIPPINCOTT COMPANY TO USE THE MEASURED
DRAWINGS OF MR. ALBERT SIMONS. THEY
ALSO WISH TO RECORD THE VALUED ASSIS-
TANCE OF MESSRS. JOHN BENNETT, C. C.
WILSON, F. A. I. A., D. E. HUGER SMITH,
FREDERICK H. HORLBECK, J. A. McCORMACK,
JOSEPH E. JENKINS, WILLIAM G. MAZYCK, PROF.
J. H. EASTERBY, OF THE COLLEGE OF CHARLES-
TON; CHARLES H. WHITAKER, EDITOR OF THE
JOURNAL OF THE AMERICAN INSTITUTE OF
ARCHITECTS; MISS ALICE R. H. SMITH, MRS.
G. E. HOFFMAN, MISS ELLEN M. FITZSIMONS, OF
THE CHARLESTON LIBRARY; MISS MABEL L.
WEBBER, OF THE SOUTH CAROLINA HISTOR-
ICAL SOCIETY. TO MESSRS. TEBBS & KNELL
ARE DUE ESPECIAL THANKS FOR THEIR IN-
VALUABLE COLLABORATION IN THE MAKING
OF THE PHOTOGRAPHS.

THE EARLY ARCHITECTURE OF
CHARLESTON

Edited by
ALBERT SIMONS, A.I.A.
and
SAMUEL LAPHAM, Jr., A.I.A.

with an introduction by
SAMUEL GAILLARD STONEY

UNIVERSITY OF SOUTH CAROLINA PRESS
Columbia, South Carolina

PREFACE TO THE SECOND EDITION

In 1926 Charles Harris Whitaker, then Editor of the *Journal* of the American Institute of Architects, conceived of an ambitious project. The Press of the Institute was to publish a series of volumes covering the architectural heritage of the eastern half of the United States —a series to be known as *The Octagon Library of Early American Architecture*. The word "Octagon" referred to the Octagon House in Washington, once the home of President and Mrs. James Madison and for many years the headquarters of the A.I.A. Whitaker selected Charleston as the subject for the first volume because of the great number of early buildings of distinction which had survived the devastations of wars, hurricanes, fires, and earthquakes.

The compilers of this volume had already published in *Architectural Forum* (1923-1926) and in *Architectural Record* (1924) a series of articles on the dwelling houses, civic and industrial buildings, churches, and ironwork of Charleston. We had at our disposal a considerable collection of measured drawings of the eighteenth-century buildings and early maps of that peninsular city. Because of the generous number of photographs authorized we were able to make a highly representative showing of the best architecture that still survived. The text was reduced to a minimum as we felt that the purpose of the book was to present a vista of the evolution of taste from the mid-eighteenth to the mid-nineteenth centuries— something to be visually enjoyed without the distractions of literary comment. Dates were considered of prime importance in order to place each building in chronological sequence.

As a pioneering work, this book undoubtedly had the defects associated with such efforts. Many notable interiors of dwellings, then unknown to us, have since been rescued from neglect and deterioration and would be included were this work undertaken today. On the other hand, some of the buildings shown have been demolished.

Prior to publication in 1927, we wrote to Samuel G. Stoney, Jr., then living in New York, and invited him to write a foreword for us. Quite cheerfully, he wrote an introduction, "Charleston and Her People."

This book was not only the work of Albert Simons and Samuel Lapham but there were also additional measured drawings prepared by A. T. S. Stoney and Albert Graeser and the wealth of illustrations skillfully photographed by Tebbs and Knell. Most important of all was the enthusiasm and encouragement of Charles Harris Whitaker. Because of the collaborative nature of this work the compilers considered it proper to assume the title of editors rather than authors though they had the responsibility of assembling the various contributions into one harmonious whole linked together by their text.

The Octagon Library of Early American Architecture, Volume I: Charleston, South Carolina, came off the press in the spring of 1927; it was not advertised except in the *Journal* of the Institute and its existence was not generally known.

Scarcely two years later the economy of the country fell into the disarray of the Great Depression and the architectural profession suffered more distress than any other. Whitaker's dream of an "Octagon Library" became only a nostalgic memory. Yet it did not wholely die. As the depression deepened the Park Service of the Department of the Interior initiated a relief program for unemployed architects and draughtsmen and paid them for measuring, drawing, and recording the nature and history of the earlier buildings throughout the country. This program was known as the Historic American Building Survey. The depression ended before the task was finished, and the work of the H.A.B.S. continues with fewer but more expert workers.

In 1948 when the first issue of this book was almost exhausted, we requested the board of directors of the A.I.A. to sell the publication rights and unsold copies of the book to the Carolina Art Association, which they graciously did. The Art Association bound the few remaining unbound copies and quickly sold them, but never had sufficient funds to bring out a second edition.

Under the stimulus of the Tricentennial Year the University of South Carolina Press has undertaken an ambitious program of publication and republication of significant works on the history and culture of South Carolina. The Press has seen fit to reprint this book under the new title of *The Early Architecture of Charleston*, with the approbation and blessing of its former guardian the Carolina Art Association.

ALBERT SIMONS, F.A.I.A., AND SAMUEL LAPHAM, F.A.I.A.

CONTENTS

GABRIEL MANIGAULT · 1758-1809

CHARLESTON AND HER PEOPLE

CLUE to the character of Charleston and her people is to remember that during their period of growth and greatest importance they were essentially of the eighteenth century. It was then that their culture crystallized, and their mode of thought, their institutions, and their very pronunciation keep the flavor of the age. From that time they preserved the tradition of the classic, with its intellectual freedom, its moral tolerance, its discipline in matters of etiquette, its individualism, and the spirit of logic which elsewhere largely perished in the romantic movement.

No city was more intimately a part of its surrounding country, and none more influenced by it. Its citizenship, like that of Rome, was widespread, practically embracing the planter population of the South Carolina "low country" (as the coastal section is called); but in this case the transient countrymen-citizens were the most powerful element in the community, and it was due to these great conservatives that the town never became a mere place of traders and professional men, but kept a mental breadth and social conscience almost unhampered by business.

Rice was the great crop of the region, and the rice plantation, with its scourge of malaria in summer, its systematized negro labor, and its rich harvests, bred a class of wealthy nomads, forced to leave their homes in the summer and well able to afford a long holiday in the winter. In the summer many of these families came to town, and during the months of the winter season, everyone that counted in the "low country" came also. There was a very strong aristocratic feeling among these people and they dominated the community. While the attempt of the Lords Proprietors, with Locke's Constitution as a guide, had failed to set an hereditary titled class, the spirit, due to the very life they led, was very present. A man who counted his negroes by fifties and his acres by thousands fell easily into the mood. With material fit to form such a class, and the Whig aristocracy as a natural model, they were not bad rulers.

The "low country" was a fascinating place to live in. The climate is pleasant the year round. Never too cold in winter to keep men within doors, it is sharp enough to temper their blood between summers. Its summer days, refreshed by regular changes of wind from the great water-courses, were never too severe to prevent Europeans from working in the fields. The malaria made the negro the agricultural laborer exclusively. Its fine native flora made it a land of delight for the gardener and the botanist. Rochefoucauld-Liancourt said that a park might be easily formed there by cutting the trees that were not necessary, the rest being fine enough, and a garden might be come at as easily. With the climatic necessity for large yards about the house, the town became a place of gardens. Two popular exotics immortalize her botanists, for poinsettias and gardenias are named for Charlestonians. Near enough to the tropics to allow their more hardy plants to pass the winter in the open, the climate is not too warm for most of those of the temperate zone. Every garden has its figs and pomegranates, its peaches and oranges, its oleanders and myrtles, azaleas and camellias, acacias and jujubes, and roses. The country itself gave yellow jessamine, wild rose, live oak, and magnolia.

The institutions of the place are hard to date. Two wars, with great destruction of records, make positive statement of antiquity a rather dubious matter. Certainly the museum was the earliest in the colonies; whether the race-course and theatre, the library society, were the first or only the second or third is questionable. That there should be a question shows what a rapid growth in culture the early community made, and the list of activities shows the broadness of the culture. In music it had a society of gentlemen-amateurs who gave concerts from sometime before the Revolution. The society still exists, but it gives only balls now.

The region had never been one which needed or desired industrialism. When the Revolution came, the Charlestonians joined the movement more from a desire for abstract justice than from any economic pressure such as brought more northerly colonies into the struggle. These fought for principles and won, only to find themselves engaged in a struggle of the same sort which was to last the better part of a century and end in defeat. When the power to tax gravitated to the northern states, it was used, as it is always used, by the industrialists, to exact tribute from the agricultural minority. Then, as now, the tariff was the method used. Finally, South Carolina protested. Unfortunately for her and for the country, the strongest President between Washington and Lincoln was in the White House. Jackson fought the Nullification Ordinance and there was a compromise. It was a mere truce, for the struggle went on and was further embittered by the slavery question.

Charleston took a leading part in all of these struggles; they were all-absorbing;

there was no other road for talent, no other expression for genius; for three generations everything was thrown into the fight. Here, at last, was signed the ordinance which dissolved the old union forever, and here was fired the first shot in justification of that ordinance.

If these people did nothing else worthy of memorial, they set up in their city records of a society and a civilization, drawn from an older time, preserved with anxious care, and transmitted with accretions of beauty and fitness from generation to generation.

SAMUEL GAILLARD STONEY

HOUSES OF
CORAL STONE.
ALBERT SIMONS

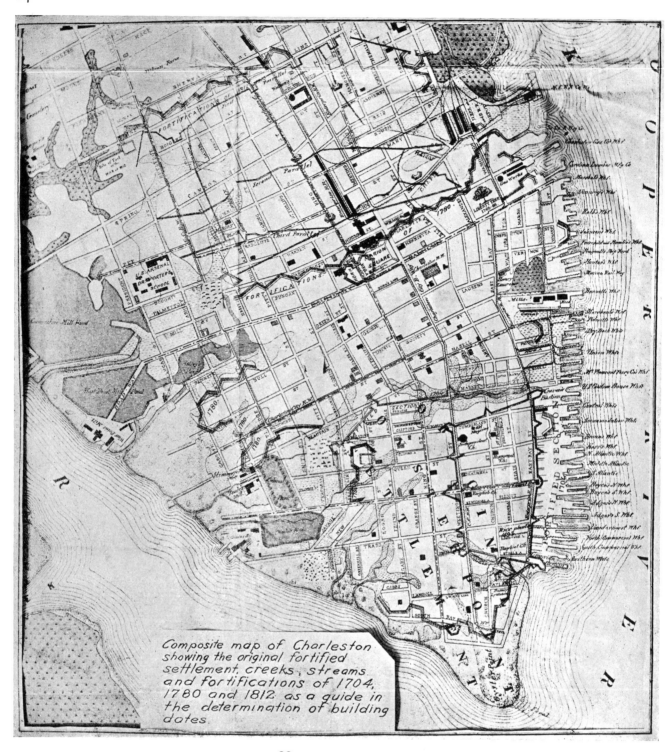

Composite map of Charleston showing the original fortified settlement, creeks, streams and fortifications of 1704, 1780 and 1812 as a guide in the determination of building dates.

CHARLESTON—A COMPOSITE MAP MADE IN 1883

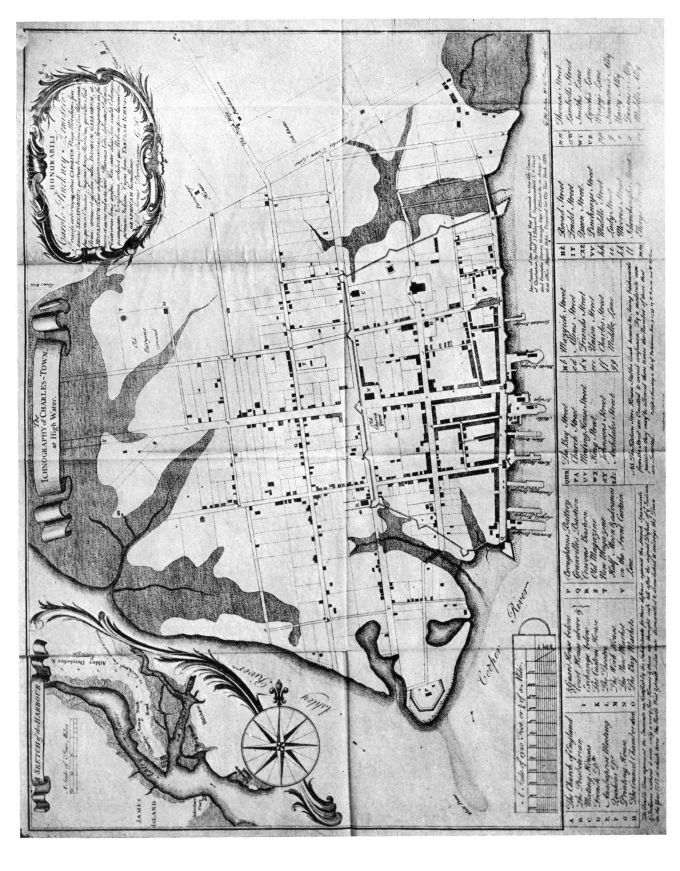

CHARLESTON—1739

THE PRE-REVOLUTIONARY PERIOD

THE FIRST settlement of Charleston was in 1670, on the west bank of the Ashley River, at Albemarle Point. Ten years later the settlement was moved to the present site, on the peninsula between the Ashley and Cooper rivers, as being a more desirable position. These first settlers were English, but after the revocation of the Edict of Nantes (1685) they were joined by considerable numbers of Huguenots whose refuge in the colony had been graciously encouraged by King Charles II, with the expectation that they would engage in the culture of silk, oil, and wine, in order that British commerce might become independent of France for its supply of these staple luxuries.

Today, in searching for evidences of French influence in the architecture of the city, it is difficult to point out anything that is indisputably Gallic, for what is not English has rather more of a Dutch character. This may derive from the fact that some of the Huguenot settlers had taken refuge in Holland before coming to the colony; also, in the alluvial coast lands of Carolina, not stone, as in France, but brick, the traditional building material of the Low Countries, was available and extensively used. However, the French strain in the people of coastal Carolina manifested itself in an appreciation of and a desire for the monumental and judiciously proportioned in architecture, and it is the presence of this character in so many buildings of comparatively small dimensions that gives the city much of its individuality and charm.

The period of greatest prosperity in Colonial times seems to have been the four middle decades of the eighteenth century. The planters were in the large majority, with much smaller numbers of merchant-traders and artisans. The cultivation of rice was started in the seventeenth century, and of indigo in the first half of the eighteenth. The original small grants were soon absorbed into large holdings and the plantation system was modeled on that of the older British colony in the Barbadoes, establishing a decidedly aristocratic basis of society. Although the planters were extremely prosperous, the largest permanent fortunes were amassed by the merchants, who were sometimes planters as well and men of highly diversified interest and great ability. Their staple exports were rice, deerskins, and indigo, with some pork, beef, and lumber. The deerskins, supplied by Indian trade, came from a vast territory extending even west of the Blue Ridge Mountains. The principal imports were rum, beer, wine, Guinea negroes, and indentured white servants, as well as a great variety of manufactured commodities. The necessities of the growing agriculture created a constant demand for black labor, which the slave-trade was ever ready to supply, despite constant legislative efforts of the colony to restrict the traffic. Very little local capital was invested in the building or ownership of large ships, and just before the Revolution there were but twelve Carolina-built vessels in use between Charleston and Europe. With the exception of some interchange, with Portugal, of rice for Madeira, the greater part of European trade was with England; this, with considerable commerce with the West Indies, but very little with the northern colonies, accounts for the architectural influence of trade.

The majority of the population was about equally divided in its allegiance to the Church of England and the Presbyterian Church; the remainder, mostly Baptists, with a very small number of Quakers and a few Sfardic Jews. The Church of England, being established by law, enjoyed the greatest power and prestige, but from the beginning of the colony, with Locke's Constitution, "Jews, heathens, and dissenters" were permitted a religious tolerance rare in those times. Hence, the great variety of ecclesiastical buildings erected to serve a comparatively small community:

CHURCH AND DENOMINATION OF TODAY	DATE OF ERECTION		
	1st Phase	2nd Phase	3d Phase
St. Philip's Episcopal	1681–90	1712	1835
St. Michael's Episcopal		1752 (a)	
St. Paul's Episcopal		1811 (a)	
French Huguenot	1681–90	1805–28	1844
Congregational (b)		1729	1804
St. John's Lutheran	1759	1815	
St. Mary's Catholic	1789	1793	1838
First Baptist	1699–1700	1746	1822
Hasell Street Synagogue	1750	1792	1838
First Presbyterian	1734 (c)	1814	
Second Presbyterian		1811 (d)	
Westminster Presbyterian			1850
Bethel Methodist		1797 (e)	1853
Spring Street Methodist			1858 (e)
Unitarian		1772 (f)	1852

(a) Offshoot of St. Philip's Episcopal.
(b) Originally Presbyterian, becoming Congregational with the withdrawal of the Presbyterians in 1734.
(c) Formed by the withdrawal mentioned under (b).
(d) Offshoot of First Presbyterian.
(e) Descendant of Cumberland Methodist Church (1787), third phase of which was burned in 1861.
(f) Originally a branch of the Congregational Church.

The architects of colonial times were essentially operative builders trained, by the long-established traditions of their craft, to a more or less sensitive feeling for the proprieties of design as well as to a knowledge of the necessities of construction. They were further assisted by those invaluable handbooks and builders' "treasuries" wherein were to be found a choice of several solutions to most of the architectural problems encountered in the general practice of the day. To this school belongs Ezra Waite, "Civil Architect, House-builder in general and Carver, from London," whose exquisite craftsmanship is to be admired in the Miles Brewton House. More monumental and of greater scope was the work of the Horlbeck brothers, John Adam and Peter, masons from Plauen, in Saxony. John learned his trade in Berlin under Christian Buckholtz, and then worked as a journeyman in Copenhagen, Riga, St. Petersburg, and Woolwich, on a variety of civil and military establishments. Finally, after many adventures on land and sea, the two brothers settled in Charleston where they became the leading builders and established a business that was continued with distinction by several generations of the name.

There were, however, besides the professional builders, others who, upon occasion, applied themselves to architecture, for the plans of St. Michael's Church were furnished by a "Mr. Gibson," whose identity we have been unable to verify, and "Mr. Samuel Cardy, the ingenious architect, undertook and completed the building." We know of no other buildings by either of these masters.

Of the very earliest buildings of the colony nothing truly authentic remains. The city has experienced five great recorded fires (1700, 1740, 1778, 1838, 1861), ten or more destructive hurricanes, and devastating earthquakes in 1811 and 1886.

The oldest dwelling houses, with few exceptions, that have come down to us hardly antedate 1740, the second of the great fires. These are of a distinct type which persisted, with little modification, until about 1760. They are built with rather thick brick walls covered with stucco made of burnt oyster-shell lime. In some instances this stucco is evidently later work, for where it has spalled it displays a brick wall laid in Flemish bond with carefully pointed joints. Unlike the later houses, the first floor is only about two feet above the grade. When piazzas occur, they appear to be considerably later additions, arising from the effort to adapt the north European type of dwelling to a subtropical climate. The street front is not always in rigid symmetry, as the doorway or a wrought-iron balcony under a second-story window may be off center, according to the requirements of the interior disposition. The drawing-room is on the second story overlooking the street, and all the more important rooms are paneled. Mouldings are bold and simple and of limited variety. Where the original mantels have been preserved there is but little carved ornament. While the street frontage of these houses is often narrow, the lots are usually deep, owing to the large blocks formed by the layout of streets; thus each piece of property constituted a large messuage. Behind the privacy of a high garden-wall of lichen-covered brick, the house, with its additions and dependencies of kitchen, washroom, servants' quarters, and stables, recedes in rambling perspective, losing itself in an overgrown garden where fig trees and pomegranates, magnolias and oleanders clothe the faded stucco in a tissue of light and shade. Seen from the garden, these accretions of buildings have a frankness of functional expression that belongs to medieval times. Especially is this noticeable in the manner of roof intersections and the placings of chimneys and dormers. Most of the roofs have a steep pitch, adhering to the building traditions of England, the Low Countries, and northern France. Along the eaves the roof becomes perceptibly less steep, flaring out in a pleasing concave curve or "bell cast." The roof-tiles are salmon-pink, sometimes salt-glazed a deep purple-black, and glitter like bright metal when seen in the sun. In section they consist of a long concave curve with a short convex curve along one edge, so that each joint is covered by the next tile alongside; they are the same type as those commonly seen in England and Holland, and are quite different from the Mediterranean semi-cylindrical tile. That these tiles were of local manufacture is evidenced by the fact that quantities of them are still to be found in the abandoned brickyards of old plantations in this vicinity. Tiles, however, were not the earliest kind of material used for roofing, for shingle roofs are still found in place, sometimes under the tile covering. Slate roofs are also quite common, especially if the roof has dormers. The old slates are quite thick and rugged, and vary greatly in size and color. They were probably brought in cargoes from Wales, as the nearest American slate quarries are in Virginia whence the difficulties of transportation would have been insurmountable.

The shapes of the roofs show considerable variety, and it is worthy of note that several of the earlier buildings made use of the gambrel or curb roof. This type is generally associated with New England, but was also tried out here in early times and given up, no doubt because rooms so close under the roof proved to be excessively hot during the greater part of the year. Besides the gambrel roof there are several examples of the "jerkin head," in which the peak of the gable is splayed off by a third roof-plane giving it a snug and blunt expression.

MEDIEVAL
ROOF LINES

ALBERT SIMONS

JERKIN HEAD ROOF

The chimney-stacks are large, to allow for log-burning fireplaces on each floor, and flues ample enough for the free passage of a "a ro-ro boy" (chimney-sweep), as the old city ordinances required all chimneys to be swept. In almost all instances these large open fireplaces have been reduced and cribbed in with cast-iron facings of gothic design that suggest nothing so much as a frontispiece from one of the old editions of the Waverley Novels. These, of course, were ushered in with the introduction of coal-grates in the Victorian era.

An interesting detail found on many old houses is the insurance plate or fire-mark. These are oval plaques about eight by ten inches, made of cast iron or lead, bearing the insignia of the company with which the house was insured. Some of these insurance companies antedate the Revolution but most are a little later. Apart from their value historically, these plaques add a spot of interest to many a blank wall-surface.

There are two small stuccoed houses, opposite St. Philip's Church, that evidently belong to this early period. They are of especial interest as being probably the only houses now standing that are built of coral stone,[1] which was brought in as ballast from Bermuda.

Practically all these earlier dwelling-houses fall roughly into two general types —the "single-house" and the "double-house"—and examples of both types continued to be built up to the Civil War. The first has been described uniquely yet clearly as follows: "houses stand sidewaies backward into their yards and only endwaies with their gables toward the street."[2] To enter the main hall, one entered the yard and walked along the side of the main body of the house until reaching the axis of the entrance door. The double-house (usually nearly square) is entered directly from the street, the doorway being on the front axis of the building. The plans of the Robert Pringle and the Horry houses, which stand side by side and are reproduced herein, illustrate these two types better than any description.

From about 1760 to the outbreak of the Revolution, which caused the cessation of building, houses were erected of larger dimensions and greater richness of detail than formerly. The first story is raised well above grade, so that more head-room is gained in the basement, and the entrance is reached by an imposing flight of steps. This elevation of the first floor arose from the desire for greater coolness, and to lift the house above the danger of flooding

[1] We are indebted to Dean H. D. Campbell, of Washington and Lee University, for the following identification: "The stone is made up of grains of coral sand with a few grains of quartz sand loosely cemented together with carbonate of lime. I would not say that all the grains of carbonate of lime came from coral, but the stone would go under the general name of coral limestone. It is the character of stone that is found on coral islands."

[2] T. Fuller, "Worthies, Exeter."

by storm tides. The drawing-room still occurs on the second floor and is now high enough to enjoy the sea-breezes that sweep across the city and keep the air fresh and cool all during the long summers.

There was, at this time, a great regard for everything British, so that the tastes and fashions of London were adopted in the colony soon after their inception in the capital. Most of the young men of wealthy families were sent to England to be educated, and upon their return home must have desired the same amenities to which they had grown accustomed in the mother country. Instances are recorded of houses erected by London builders attracted to the colony by the opportunities for plying their trade. As a result of all this close contact, many of the houses of this period have little of that tentative and naive quality that is usually associated with colonial work but are very definitely a transplanted manifestation of English-Georgian architecture.

This is especially the case in respect to the well-proportioned paneled rooms and the dextrously carved woodwork of mantels, doors, and cornices, following frequently the elegant manner of Chippendale with rococo and Chinese motifs skillfully blended. This gay and spirited architecture ceased before Sir Peter Parker's ships (1776) appeared in the harbor to attack Fort Moultrie, and when, at last, peace was restored and prosperity gradually revived, a new manner and a different taste inspired the builders of the day.

ALBERT SIMONS

GAMBREL ROOF

ST. MICHAEL'S CHURCH—1752–61. —— GIBSON, DESIGNER

ST. MICHAEL'S CHURCH

ST. MICHAEL'S CHURCH (DECORATION IN HALF-DOME AFTER 1893)

EXCHANGE AND CUSTOM HOUSE—1767–72.   PETER AND JOHN HORLBECK, BUILDERS

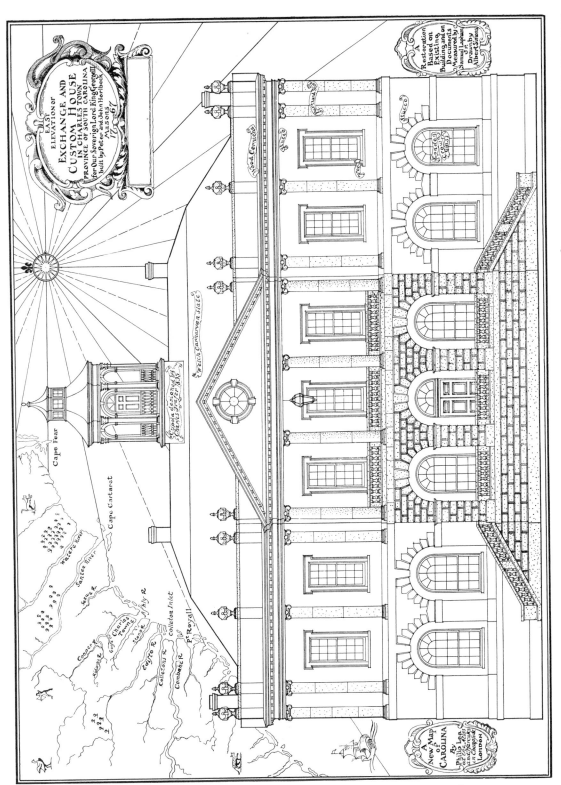

SCALE — 1″=12′, 3⁄16″

HYPOTHETICAL RESTORATION OF EAST ELEVATION OF EXCHANGE AND CUSTOM HOUSE. THIS "RESTORATION" WAS MADE BEFORE THE DISCOVERY OF THE DRAWINGS OF WILLIAM RIGBY NAYLOR IN THE HORLBECK PAPERS. IT IS IN ERROR IN THE FOLLOWING: THERE WAS NO PROJECTING PORTICO ON THIS FACADE, ONLY ENGAGED COLUMNS AS SHOWN ON PAGE 28; THE ARCADED LOWER FLOOR WAS NOT ENCLOSED WITH GLAZED SASH AND WAS REFERRED TO AS THE "PIAZZA" IN THE ARTICLE OF AGREEMENT OF 1767 BETWEEN THE HORLBECK BROTHERS AND THE COMMISSIONERS; THE WORD "PIAZZA" WAS MISINTERPRETED AS A PORTICO IN THIS DRAWING.

JACOB MOTTE'S HOUSE—1745
69 CHURCH STREET

COLONEL ROBERT BREWTON'S HOUSE—BEFORE 1733
71 CHURCH STREET

JACOB MOTTE'S HOUSE

JACOB MOTTE'S HOUSE

THE HUGER HOUSE — ABOUT 1760. 34 MEETING STREET

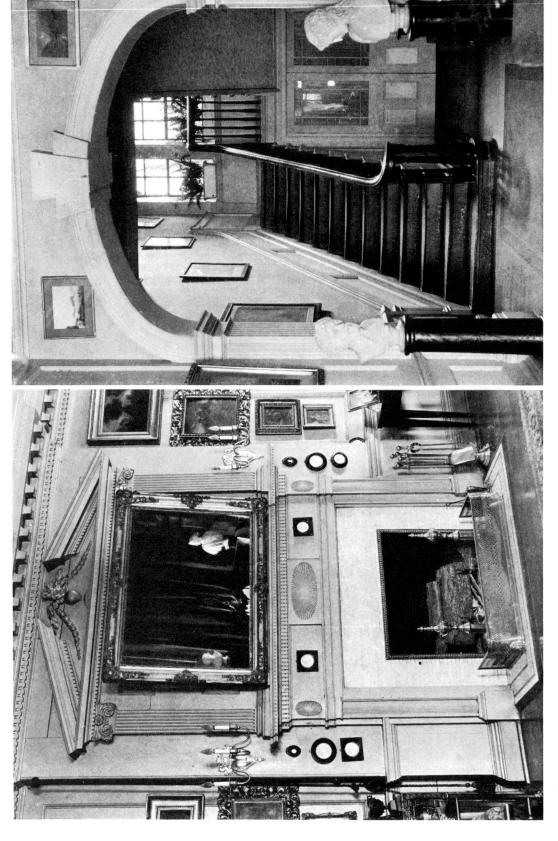

THE HUGER HOUSE

THE HUGER HOUSE

MILES BREWTON'S HOUSE—SOON AFTER 1765. 27 KING STREET

MILES BREWTON'S HOUSE

MILES BREWTON'S HOUSE

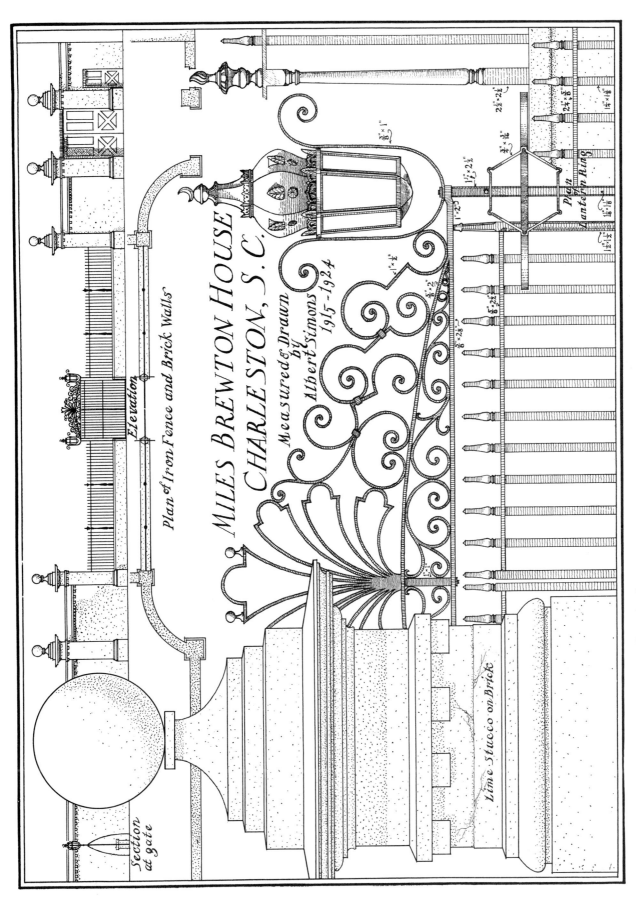

MILES BREWTON HOUSE
CHARLESTON, S.C.

Measured & Drawn
by
Albert Simons
1915–1924

Section at gate

Elevation

Plan of Iron Fence and Brick Walls

Plan of Lantern Ring

Lime Stucco on Brick

SMALL SCALE PLAN AND ELEVATION — 1″ = 14′ 9″

DETAILS — $\frac{13}{16}″$ = 1′-0″

MILES BREWTON'S HOUSE

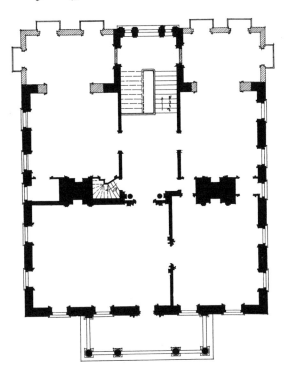

Plan of 2ᵈ floor Miles Brewton House

Scale ins 12 0 1 2 3 4 5 6 7 8 9 10 20 *feet*

DRAWN BY ALBERT SIMONS

MILES BREWTON'S HOUSE

MILES BREWTON'S HOUSE

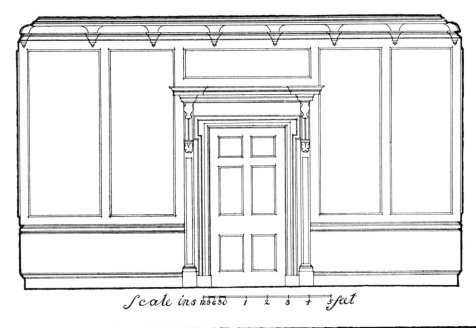

Scale ins 12 9 6 3 0 1 2 3 4 5 feet

Scale ins 12 9 6 3 0 1 2 3 4 5 feet

MILES BREWTON'S HOUSE   DRAWN BY ALBERT SIMONS

44

MILES BREWTON'S HOUSE

MILES BREWTON'S HOUSE

46

MILES BREWTON'S HOUSE

MILES BREWTON'S HOUSE

DRAWN BY ALBERT SIMONS

MILES BREWTON'S HOUSE

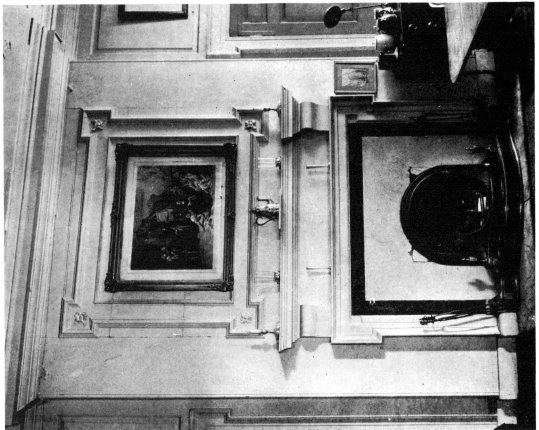

MILES BREWTON'S HOUSE

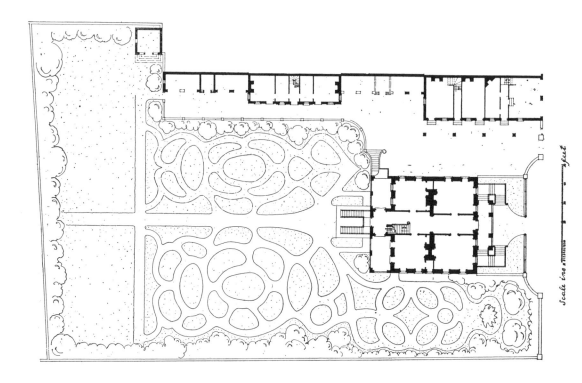

Scale in a feet — — feet

MILES BREWTON'S HOUSE. DRAWN BY ALBERT SIMONS

THE HORRY HOUSE—BETWEEN 1751 AND 1767 (PIAZZA LATER). 59 MEETING STREET

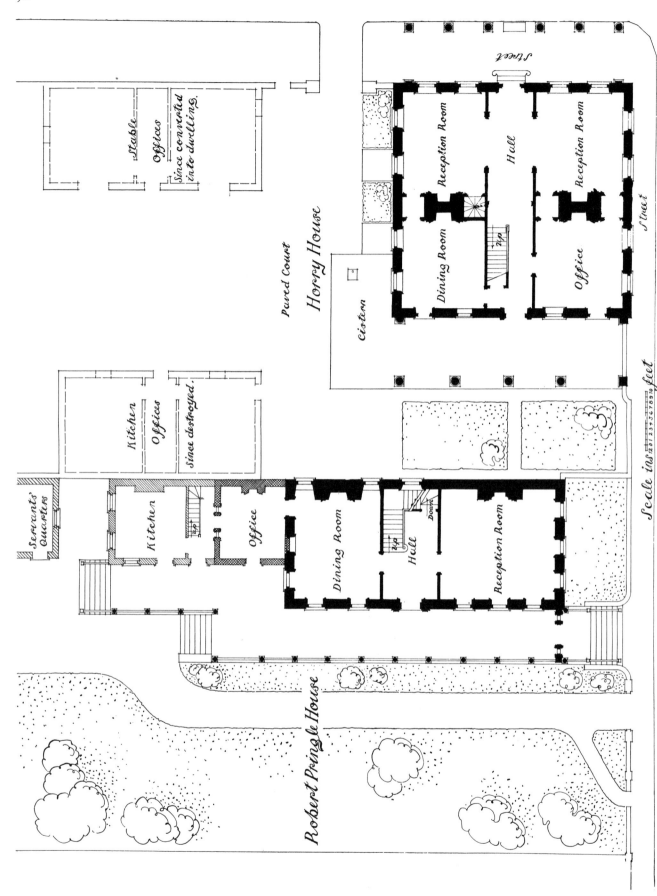

THE HORRY HOUSE

DRAWN BY ALBERT SIMONS

ROBERT PRINGLE'S HOUSE

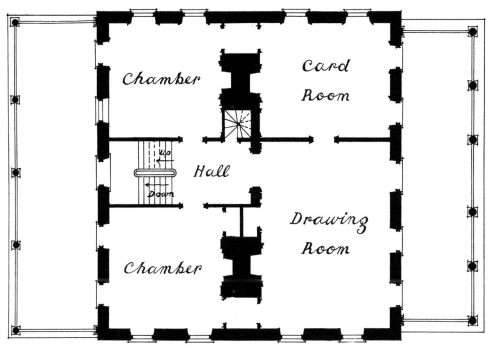

Chamber

Card
Room

Hall

Drawing
Room

Chamber

Scale ins 12 0 1 2 3 4 5 6 7 8 9 10 feet

THE HORRY HOUSE   DRAWN BY ALBERT SIMONS

THE HORRY HOUSE

Scale ins. 12 3 6 6 6 1 2 3 4 5 feet

Second Story Drawing Room of Horry House

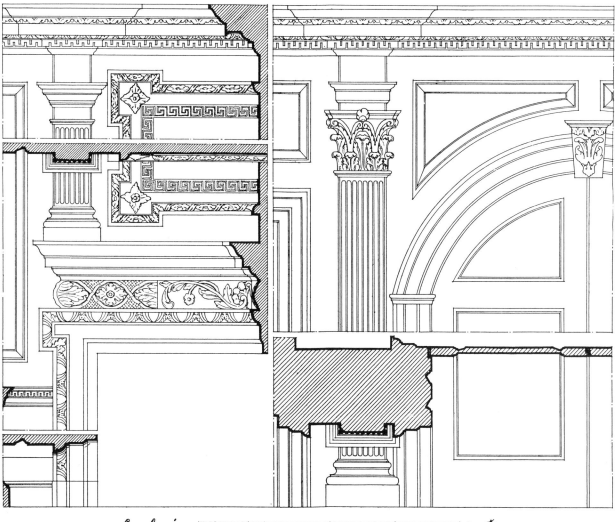

Scale ins. 9 6 3 0 1 2 3 feet

DRAWN BY ALBERT SIMONS

THE HORRY HOUSE

Scale ins. 12 9 6 3 0   1   2   3   4   5 feet

Entrance Hall of Horry House

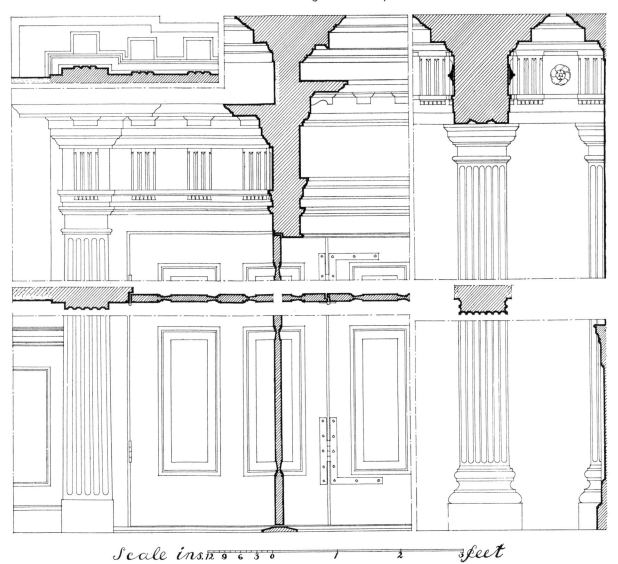

Scale ins. 12 9 6 3 0   1   2   3 feet

DRAWN BY ALBERT SIMONS

58

JUDGE ROBERT PRINGLE'S HOUSE—1774. 70 TRADD STREET

JUDGE ROBERT PRINGLE'S HOUSE

JUDGE ROBERT PRINGLE'S HOUSE

GENERAL WILLIAM WASHINGTON'S HOUSE—AFTER 1768. SOUTH BATTERY AND CHURCH STREET

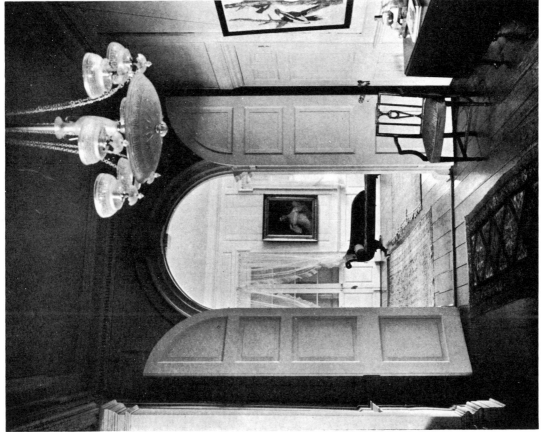

GENERAL WILLIAM WASHINGTON'S HOUSE

GENERAL WILLIAM WASHINGTON'S HOUSE

GENERAL WILLIAM WASHINGTON'S HOUSE

66

"CABBAGE ROW" (TOP). CHURCH STREET   HOUSE AT 21 CHARLES STREET (BOTTOM)

JOHN EDWARDS' HOUSE—ABOUT 1770. 15 MEETING STREET

JOHN EDWARDS' HOUSE

Scale ins 2 9 6 3 0   1   2   3 feet

Drawing Room Mantel
of
John Edwards House

Scale ins 12 11 10 9 8 7 6 5 4 3 2 1 0   3 feet

DRAWN BY ALBERT SIMONS

JOHN EDWARDS' HOUSE

JOHN EDWARDS' HOUSE

JOHN EDWARDS' HOUSE

HOUSE AT 45 QUEEN STREET

74

HOUSES IN TRADD STREET

ST. PHILIP'S CHURCH PARSONAGE — ABOUT 1770.   GLEBE STREET

HOUSE AT 25 MEETING STREET

Scale ins. 12 9 6 3 0 1 2 3 feet

HUMPHREY SOMMERS' HOUSE

DRAWN BY ALBERT SIMONS

HUMPHREY SOMMERS' HOUSE—ABOUT 1765. 128 TRADD STREET

RALPH IZARD'S HOUSE—1728 (DOORWAY IS LATER ALTERATION). 110 BROAD STREET

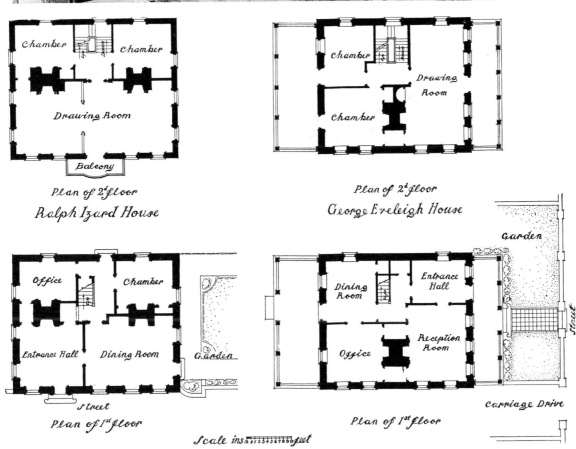

Chamber   Chamber

Drawing Room

Balcony

Plan of 2ᵈ floor
Ralph Izard House

Chamber

Drawing Room

Chamber

Plan of 2ᵈ floor
George Eveleigh House

Office   Chamber

Entrance Hall   Dining Room

Garden

Street

Plan of 1ˢᵗ floor

Garden

Dining Room   Entrance Hall

Office   Reception Room

Street

Carriage Drive

Plan of 1ˢᵗ floor

Scale ins ⌐ feet

RALPH IZARD'S HOUSE   DRAWN BY ALBERT SIMONS   GEORGE EVELEIGH'S HOUSE

GEORGE EVELEIGH'S HOUSE—1738. 39 CHURCH STREET

PINK HOUSE IN CHALMERS STREET

HOUSE AT 21 CHARLES STREET

COLONEL JOHN STUART'S HOUSE—ABOUT 1772. 104 TRADD STREET

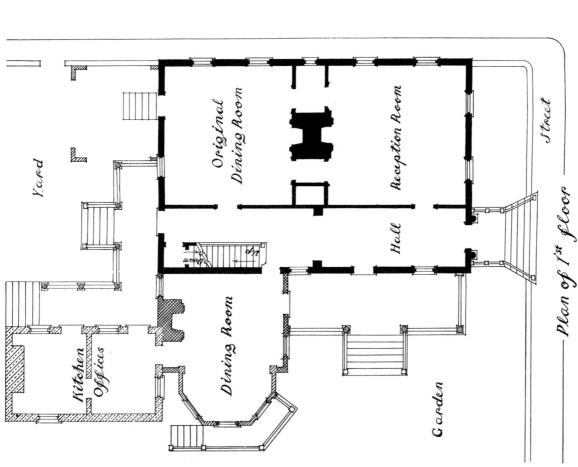

Chamber

Chamber

Drawing Room

Plan of 2ᵈ floor

Yard

Kitchen
Offices

Original
Dining Room

Dining Room

Reception Room

Hall

Garden

Street

Scale ins 121 0 1 2 3 4 5 6 7 8 9 10 feet

Plan of 1ˢᵗ floor

DRAWN BY ALBERT SIMONS

COLONEL JOHN STUART'S HOUSE—ORIGINAL PLAN IN SOLID BLACK LINES

84

COLONEL JOHN STUART'S HOUSE

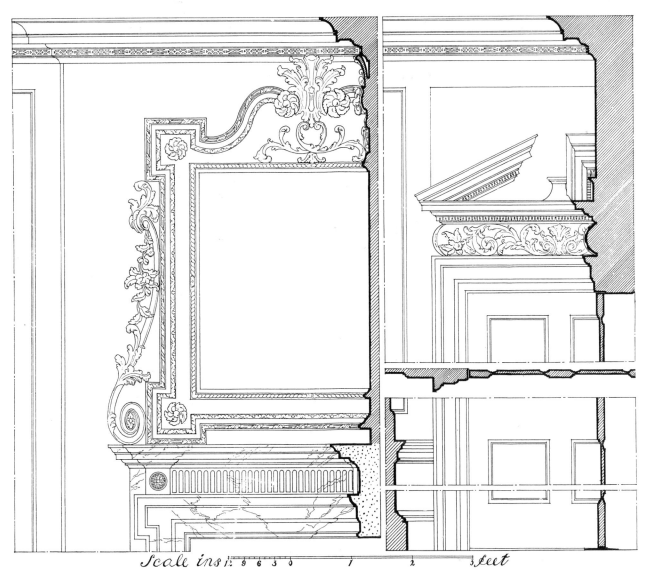

COLONEL JOHN STUART'S HOUSE—DRAWING-ROOM   DRAWN BY ALBERT SIMONS

COLONEL JOHN STUART'S HOUSE

COLONEL JOHN STUART'S HOUSE

88

STAIRWAY — HOUSE AT 45 QUEEN STREET

COLONEL JOHN STUART'S HOUSE

DANIEL BLAKE'S TENEMENTS — EASTERN HALF

SERVANTS' QUARTERS AT 45 QUEEN STREET

DANIEL BLAKE'S TENEMENTS—BETWEEN 1760 AND 1772. COURT HOUSE SQUARE

DANIEL BLAKE'S TENEMENTS

DANIEL BLAKE'S TENEMENTS—EASTERN HALF

DANIEL BLAKE'S TENEMENTS — WESTERN HALF

94

WILLIAM GIBBES' HOUSE—BEFORE 1789. 64 SOUTH BATTERY

WILLIAM GIBBES' HOUSE

WILLIAM GIBBES' HOUSE

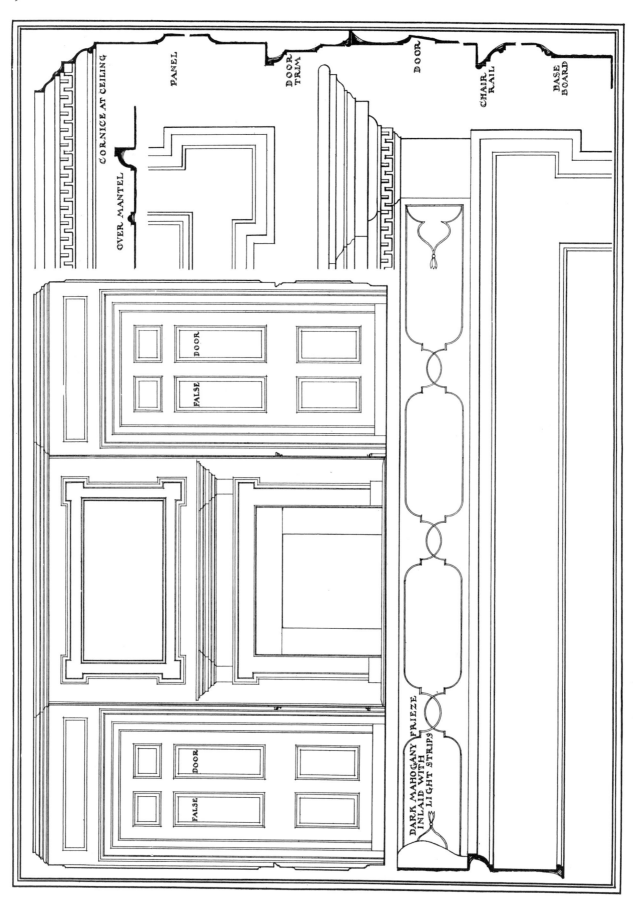

CORNICE AT CEILING

PANEL

OVER MANTEL

DOOR TRIM

DOOR

CHAIR RAIL

BASE BOARD

DOOR

FALSE

DOOR

FALSE

DARK MAHOGANY FRIEZE INLAID WITH LIGHT STRIPS

DRAWN BY ALBERT SIMONS

HOUSE AT 60 CHURCH STREET — MAHOGANY-PANELED ROOM

ELEVATION — $\frac{13}{32}$" = 1' 0".   DETAILS — $1\frac{5}{8}$" = 1' 0"

THE POST-REVOLUTIONARY PERIOD

SIR HENRY CLINTON'S MAP OF CHARLESTON — 1780

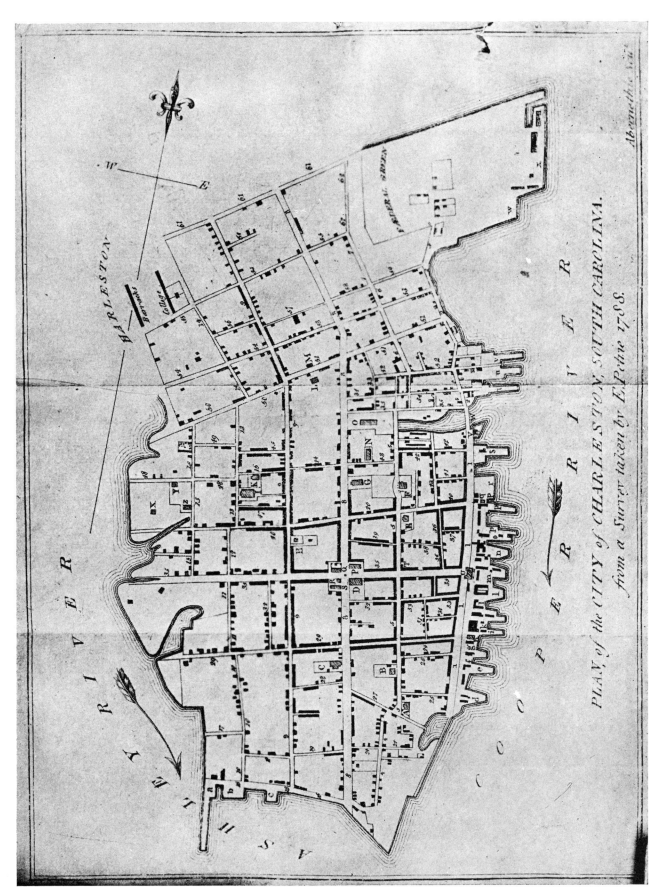

PLAN of the CITY of CHARLESTON, SOUTH CAROLINA.
from a Survey taken by E. Petrie 1788.

CHARLESTON — 1788

THE POST-REVOLUTIONARY PERIOD

URING the Revolution, Charleston became one of the chief focal points of the war-zone. After successfully resisting a combined naval and military attack in 1776, under General Clinton and Sir Peter Parker, it was swept by a destructive fire in 1778, shelled by General Prevost in 1779, and finally, after the fall of Savannah, was shut in by Clinton, with fortifications thrown across the neck of land between the two rivers and by a fleet anchored in the harbor. In 1780, after a protracted siege, General Lincoln surrendered the city to the British, who did not evacuate until December, 1782.

When the chaos of war ceased, the town presented the appearance of an armed camp. A considerable area lay within the fortifications, but there were few buildings, and several of these were barracks. In many parts of the town were large vacant spaces called "greens"; these had been used for drilling and maneuvering troops. The whole terrain was intersected by lagoons, tide marshes, and creeks navigable by small craft and spanned by bridges to connect the isolated boroughs.

Commerce and trade had disappeared; many substantial Tory citizens had fled; even the leaders of the victorious patriots had been ruined financially. There was no stable system of currency, and there was no credit available with which to start new business. Until raw products could be produced for export, extreme poverty prevailed. The production of indigo, which had been subsidized by the Crown and had been the source of much wealth, had now ceased, never to be revived. Until cotton was introduced as a staple, and the swamps along the rivers had been systematically cleared and dyked for the more general cultivation of rice, the depression continued. In 1787, water mills took the place of manual processes for cleaning and polishing the grain, effecting a greater profit. Banks were established and foreign trade, which had been formerly monopolized by Great Britain, spread to all parts of Europe. Manufactured articles needed by the entire state were imported by the merchants, while down the rivers to the wharves floated barges from the plantations, bearing vast quantities of rice, and along the miry roads plodded long defiles of ox-drawn wagons piled high with cotton from the up-country. At the shops and taverns in Broad, Elliot, and Tradd streets could be found English hardware and woolens, French silks and brandies, Canton china, Madras prints, Spanish and Portuguese wines, and Jamaica rum.

Prosperity grew with the closing of the eighteenth and the opening decades of the nineteenth century. With the outbreak of the Napoleonic Wars, following the French Revolution, the British Navy destroyed the French merchant marine, and France opened her commerce to neutrals; thus American trade prospered greatly, supplying France and the French West Indies with food-stuffs. This led to reprisals from Great Britain, reflected here by the disappearance of foreign commerce and the accumulation of raw produce, with an accompanying decline in values and loss of capital, which was further aggravated by the "State of War" that existed with France for some years. The conditions became acute prior to the War of 1812, but by 1816 hard times had passed and the town entered upon a new period of prosperity and expansion which lasted until the debacle of 1860.

It will be noted, in general, that intensive building usually follows a period of commercial activity, and that construction frequently goes forward when the tide of prosperity has reached its flood or has begun to ebb. This may be accounted for by the fact that building operations proceeded slowly in those days and considerable time was spent in preparation before the project could be commenced. With the first economic recovery following the Revolution, we note the erection of a considerable number of religious, philanthropic, and social institutions, as well as commercial and domestic buildings.

Perhaps the most gifted architect of this period was Gabriel Manigault, the third of his family in America to bear that name. He was a gentleman rice-planter of independent means who had completed his education in Geneva and London and brought home with him from England a valuable architectural library. He was the first Charleston architect in the more modern acceptance of the term, in that he prepared designs to be executed by builders. However, his equipment seems to have been more that of a cultured amateur than of the thoroughly trained professional. All of his work betrays the elegant attenuation of proportions, smallness of scale, and flatness of detail which characterize the work of the Adam Brothers and their immediate successors. He died in Philadelphia in 1809.

The dwelling-house of this period following immediately after the Revolution displays considerable ingenuity and variety of plan. Gracefully winding stairways and oval drawing-rooms indicate the influence of architects conversant with contemporary French as well as English practice.   Paneling disappears from the interiors, except as wainscoting.   Mouldings become very small in scale and of greater variety of profile.   Much reeding and channeling is resorted to, as well as composition ornament of standardized Adam types. Plaster cornices and centerpieces enrich the lofty ceilings in the main rooms. Piazzas, or open galleries, in two or three tiers, assume greater proportions and extend the entire length of the house along the western or southern exposure, shielding the house from the hot rays during the day and affording an airy retreat in the evening. Various expedients were employed to overcome the lack of unity of design which these many-storied appendages imposed. Perhaps the most successful was to reduce the columns to very slender proportions and span them with extremely flat segmental arches.   This gives the piazza frankly the character of secondary importance and emphasis and is sufficiently pleasing in appearance to be tolerated.   Later, with the advent of a more rigid classicism, the end of the piazza facing the street was sometimes walled up and treated with windows similar to those on the rest of the house.   The fallacy of this contrivance is at once apparent when the house is viewed at an angle across the garden.

These general types of buildings continued in use up to the Civil War, although, with the approach of the middle of the century, there appeared an increasing tendency towards the large in scale accompanied by the simplification and coarsening of the detail, due to the replacement of white craftsmen by negro artisans. While there is no sharp line of demarcation between the post-Revolutionary and the ante-bellum periods—for the transition is continuous—yet the final development is so far from the point of departure as to make some distinction seem appropriate.

SECOND PRESBYTERIAN CHURCH—1811

106

ST. PAUL'S CHURCH—1811–1816

IRON GATES — 1823

ST. JOHN'S LUTHERAN CHURCH — 1815–1818

ST. JOHN'S LUTHERAN CHURCH — IRON GATES
SCALE—$\frac{1\frac{1}{2}''}{32}$ = 1' 0"

DRAWN BY ALBERT SIMONS

FIRST PRESBYTERIAN CHURCH — 1814

UNITED STATES BANK — 1801 (NOW CITY HALL).   GABRIEL MANIGAULT, ARCHITECT

(TOP) CHARLESTON ORPHAN HOUSE CHAPEL — 1802. GABRIEL MANIGAULT, ARCHITECT
(BOTTOM) COURT HOUSE — BETWEEN 1788–1800. JUDGE WILLIAM DRAYTON, ARCHITECT

SOUTH CAROLINA SOCIETY HALL—1804. GABRIEL MANIGAULT, ARCHITECT
PORTICO ADDED IN 1825. FREDERICK WESNER, ARCHITECT

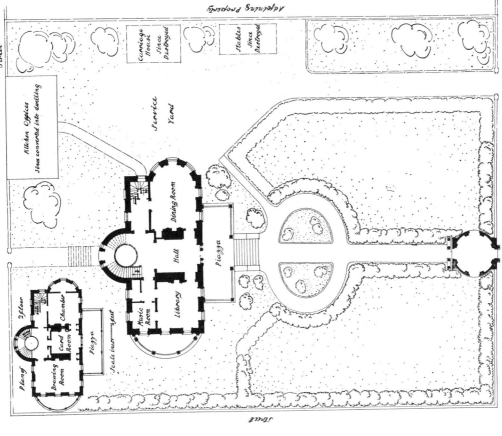

Joseph Manigault House

DRAWN BY ALBERT SIMONS

JOSEPH MANIGAULT'S HOUSE — GATE LODGE — ABOUT 1790.   GABRIEL MANIGAULT, ARCHITECT

SCALE of DETAIL 0 1 2 3 4 5 6 7 8 9 10 11 12 INCHES

Section D-D

Section A-A

Section E-E

Section B-B

Section C-C

Street Elevation

Garden Elevation

Plan Section

SCALE 1 2 3 4 5 6 Feet

JOSEPH MANIGAULT'S HOUSE — GATE LODGE   DRAWN BY A. T. S. STONEY

JOSEPH MANIGAULT'S HOUSE — GATE LODGE

DRAWING-ROOM

ELIHU HALL BAY'S HOUSE—SERVANTS' QUARTERS—1785
76 MEETING STREET

Wall Line

Wall Line

Section A-A.

Section of Wainscot.

Scale 6 inches

Wall Line

Section of Cornice

Section B-B.

Wall Line

A   B

B

A

Scale of Trim
INCHES
0 1 2 3 4 5 6

Scale of Doorway
FEET
12 9 6 3 0   1   2

THE MISSROON HOUSE — 1789–95.   EAST BATTERY

DRAWN BY A. T. S. STONEY

JUDGE KING'S HOUSE—BEFORE 1806. 24 GEORGE STREET

Plan Section A-A

Folding
Blinds

Chair rail.

Wood

Plaster

Wall

Arch & Cornice Profile Section on ℄

Scale of Detail
Inches.

0   1   2   3   4

Scale   12 9 6 3 0   1   2   3   4   Feet.

JUDGE KING'S HOUSE — PALLADIAN WINDOW   DRAWN BY A. T. S. STONEY

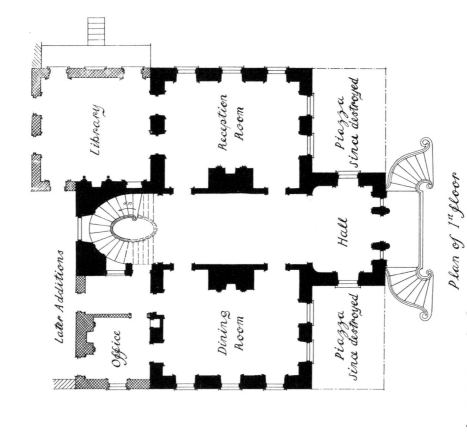

Later Additions

Office

Library

Reception Room

Dining Room

Piazza since destroyed

Hall

Piazza since destroyed

Plan of 1st floor

Scale in 9 8 7 6 5 4 3 2 1 0 1 2 3 4 5 6 7 8 9 10 *feet*

DRAWN BY ALBERT SIMONS

JUDGE KING'S HOUSE

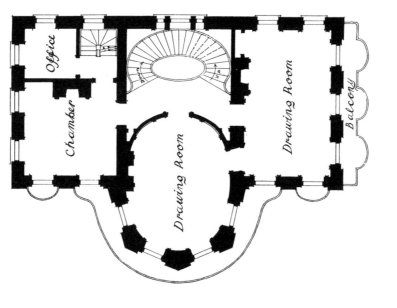

Office

Chamber

Drawing Room

Drawing Room

Balcony

Plan of 2d floor

NATHANIEL RUSSELL'S HOUSE

NATHANIEL RUSSELL'S HOUSE — BEFORE 1811. 51 MEETING STREET

NATHANIEL RUSSELL'S HOUSE

SERVANTS' QUARTERS

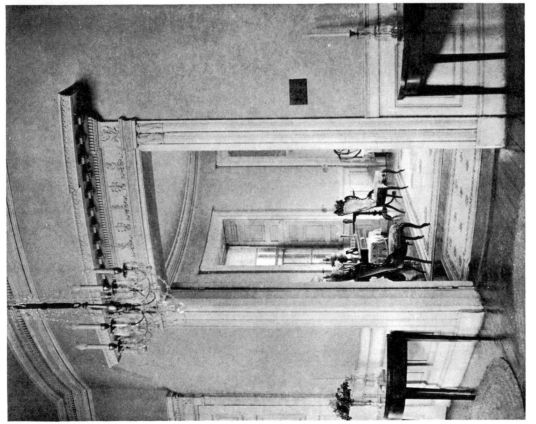

NATHANIEL RUSSELL'S HOUSE

THE MIDDLETON-PINCKNEY HOUSE—ABOUT 1797. 14 GEORGE STREET

Scale of Plan: 0 5 10 15 20 25 30 Feet

Scale of Doorway 0 2 4 6 8 10 12 14 16 18 20 Inches

THE MIDDLETON-PINCKNEY HOUSE—FRONT DOORWAY AND FIRST FLOOR PLAN.
DRAWN BY A. T. S. STONEY

THE MIDDLETON-PINCKNEY HOUSE

WILLIAM BLACKLOCK'S HOUSE — ABOUT 1800. 14 BULL STREET

WILLIAM BLACKLOCK'S HOUSE

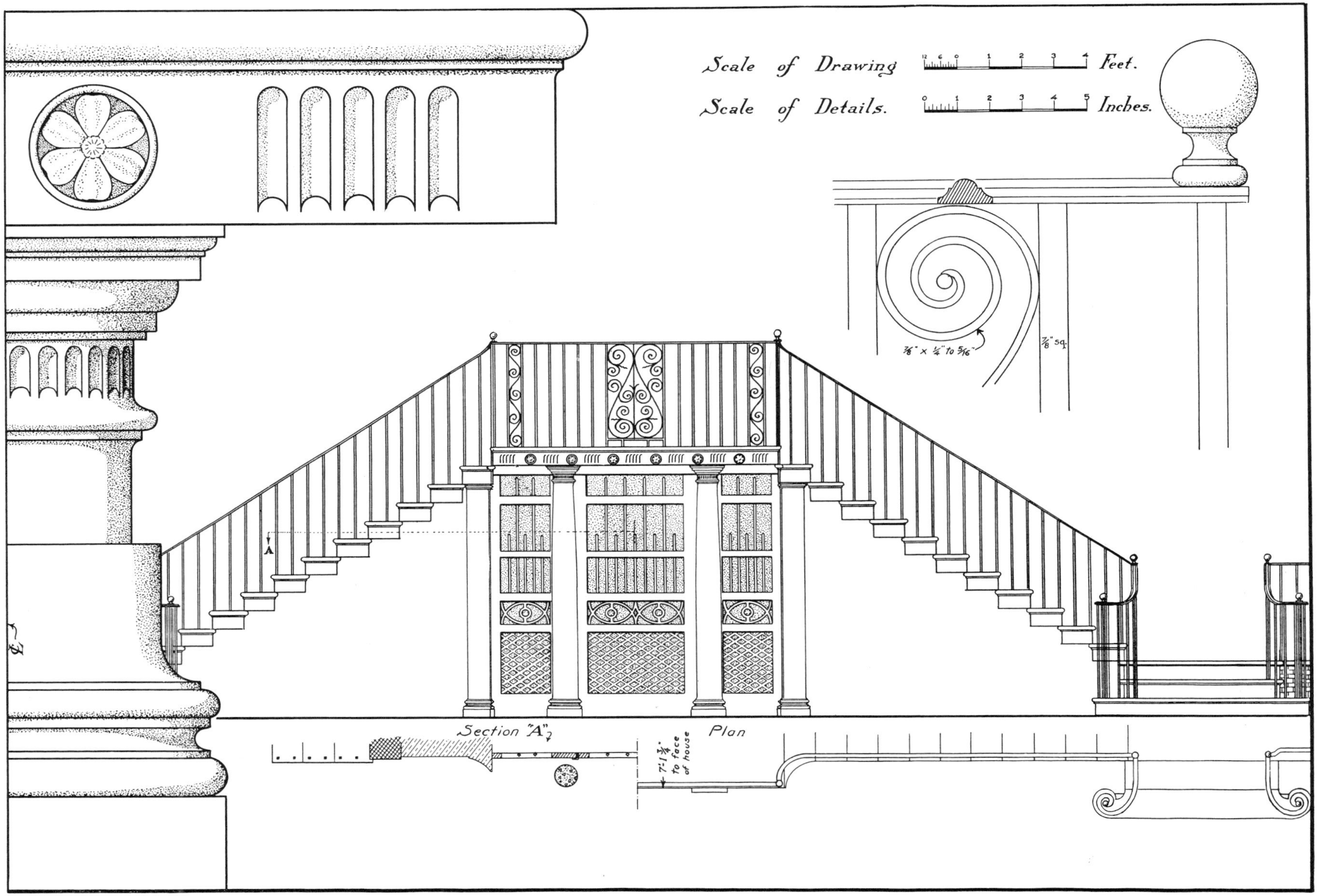

Scale of Drawing

Feet.

Scale of Details.

Inches.

Plan

Section "A"

WILLIAM BLACKLOCK'S HOUSE—FRONT STEPS

DRAWN BY A. T. S. STONEY

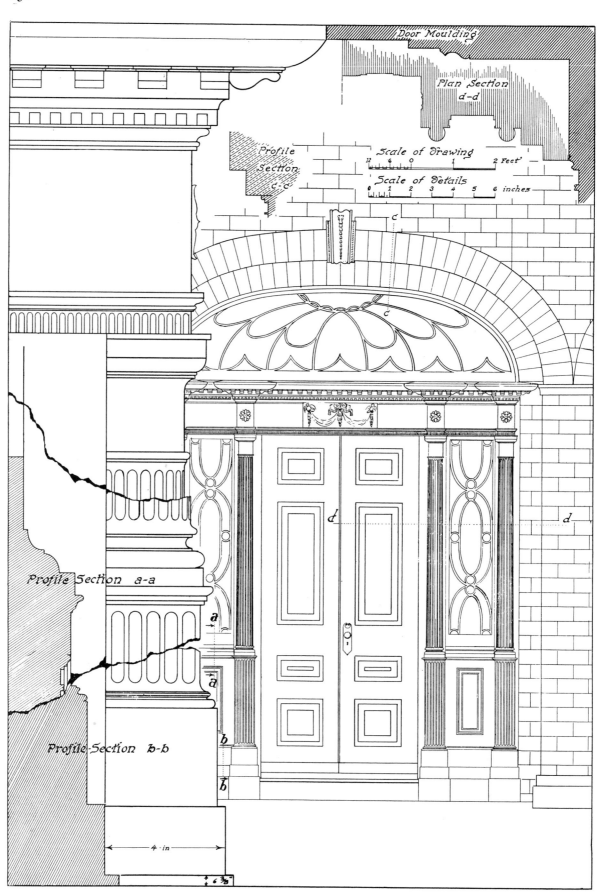

Door Moulding

Plan Section
d-d

Profile
Section
c-c

Scale of Drawing
12 6 0   1   2 Feet

Scale of Details
0 1 2 3 4 5 6 inches

c

c

c

d

d

Profile Section a-a

a

a

a

b

Profile Section b-b

b

b

4·in

6⅜

WILLIAM BLACKLOCK'S HOUSE—FRONT DOOR

DRAWN BY A. T. S. STONEY

WILLIAM BLACKLOCK'S HOUSE

132

A GATE ON ORANGE STREET AT THE CORNER OF BROAD STREET

WILLIAM BLACKLOCK'S HOUSE — SERVANTS' QUARTERS

DANIEL RAVENEL'S HOUSE — SERVANTS' QUARTERS — ABOUT 1800. 68 BROAD STREET

· THIRD · FLOOR · PLAN ·   · ATTIC · FLOOR · PLAN ·

· FIRST · FLOOR · PLAN ·   · SECOND · FLOOR · PLAN ·

VANDERHORST ROW — 1800.   EAST BAY   DRAWN BY SAMUEL LAPHAM, JR.

VANDERHORST ROW

HOUSE AT 92 CHURCH STREET — COACH HOUSE AT LEFT

JOSIAH SMITH'S HOUSE — 1800. 7 MEETING STREET

HOUSE AT 8 MEETING STREET

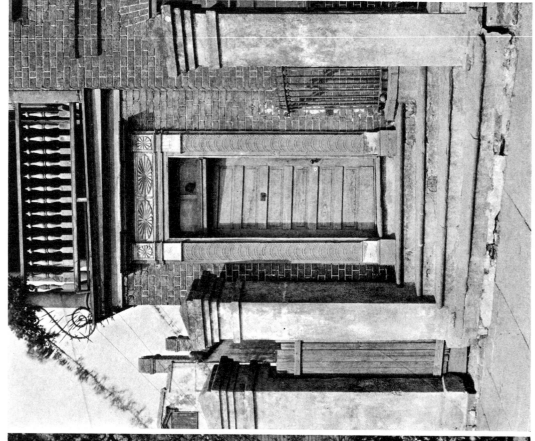

HOUSE IN EAST BAY

WILLIAM DRAYTON'S HOUSE—1820–22. 6 GIBBES STREET

WILLIAM DRAYTON'S HOUSE

WILLIAM DRAYTON'S HOUSE (TOP)
WILLIAM AIKEN'S HOUSE — BEFORE 1827. 456 KING STREET (BOTTOM)

DANIEL RAVENEL'S HOUSE—ABOUT 1800. 68 BROAD STREET

GEORGE EDWARDS' HOUSE (TOP).   COACH HOUSE (BOTTOM)

GEORGE EDWARDS' HOUSE—BEFORE 1786. 14 LEGARÉ STREET

GEORGE EDWARDS' HOUSE

GEORGE EDWARDS' HOUSE

GEORGE EDWARDS' HOUSE

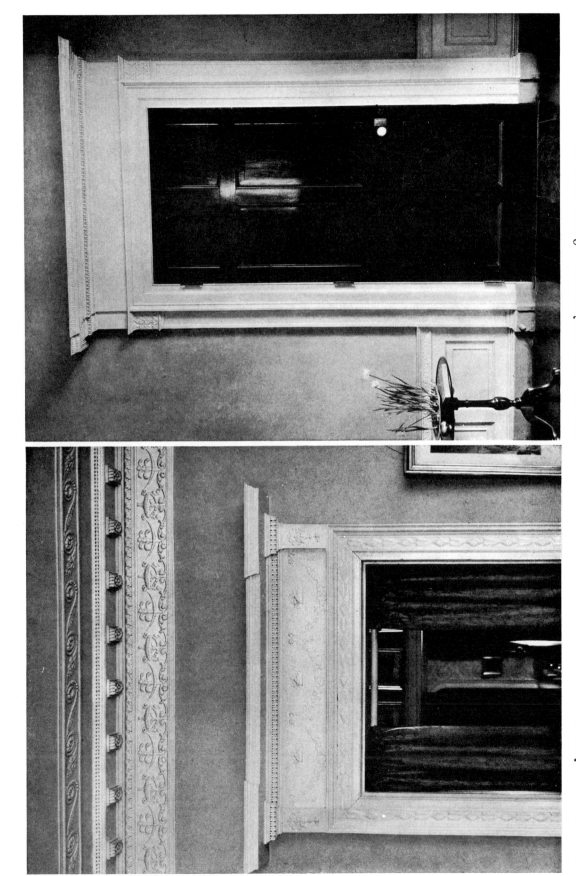

HENRY MANIGAULT'S HOUSE.   18 MEETING STREET

GEORGE EDWARDS' HOUSE

148

JONATHAN LUCAS' HOUSE. CALHOUN STREET — WEST END

HENRY MANIGAULT'S HOUSE

HOUSE AT 116 CHURCH STREET

HOUSE AT 114 CHURCH STREET

JONATHAN LUCAS' HOUSE

HOUSE AT 13 CHURCH STREET

HOUSE AT 55 EAST BAY

HOUSE AT 20 MONTAGUE STREET

THOMAS GRANGE SIMONS' HOUSE — BEFORE 1818. 128 BULL STREET (TOP)
HOUSE AT 71 ANSON STREET (BOTTOM)

HOUSE AT 173 RUTLEDGE AVENUE (TOP)
GOVERNOR THOMAS BENNETT'S HOUSE — LUCAS STREET (BOTTOM)

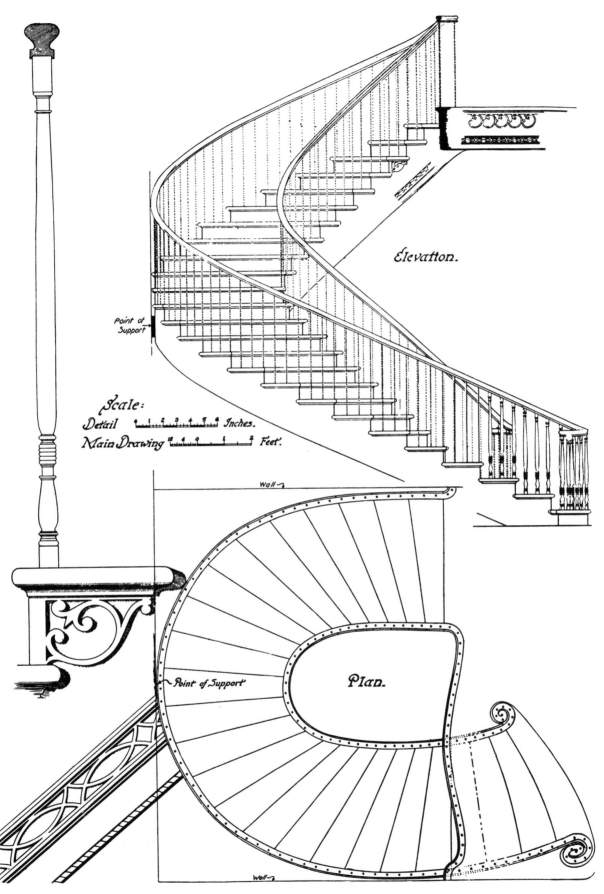

Point of
Support

Elevation.

Scale:
Detail ⌊╌╌╌╌╌╌╌╌╌⌋ Inches.
Main Drawing ⌊╌╌╌╌╌╌╌╌⌋ Feet.

Wall

Point of Support

Plan.

Wall

GOVERNOR BENNETT'S HOUSE — THE WINDING STAIRWAY

DRAWN BY A. T. S. STONEY

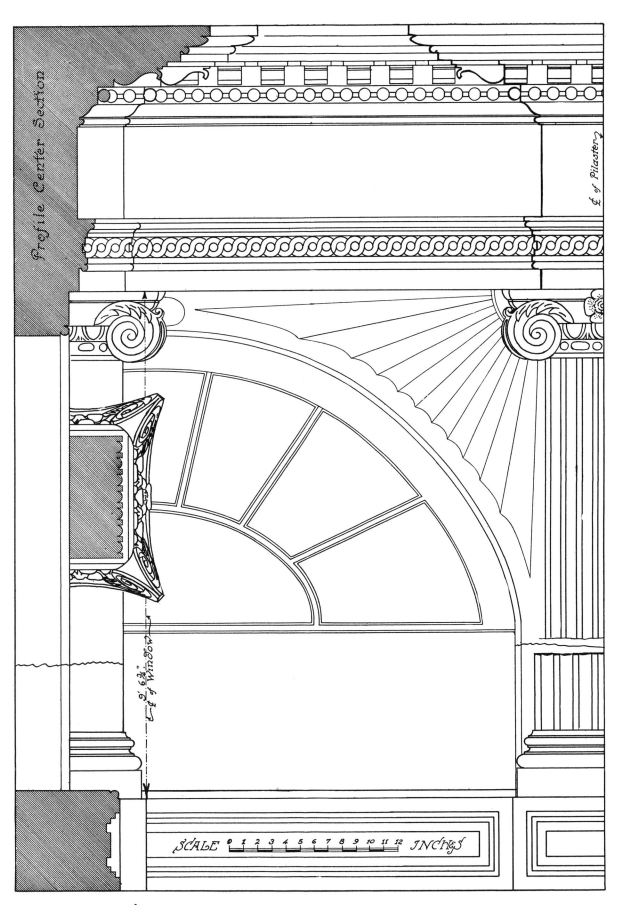

Profile Center Section

℄ of Pilaster

2' 6¾" ℄ of Window

SCALE 0 1 2 3 4 5 6 7 8 9 10 11 12 INCHES

GOVERNOR BENNETT'S HOUSE — WINDOW ON THE STAIRWAY   DRAWN BY A. T. S. STONEY

GOVERNOR THOMAS BENNETT'S HOUSE

GOVERNOR THOMAS BENNETT'S HOUSE

GOVERNOR THOMAS BENNETT'S HOUSE

HOUSE AT 21 CHARLES STREET

THE MAGWOOD HOUSE—39 SOUTH BATTERY

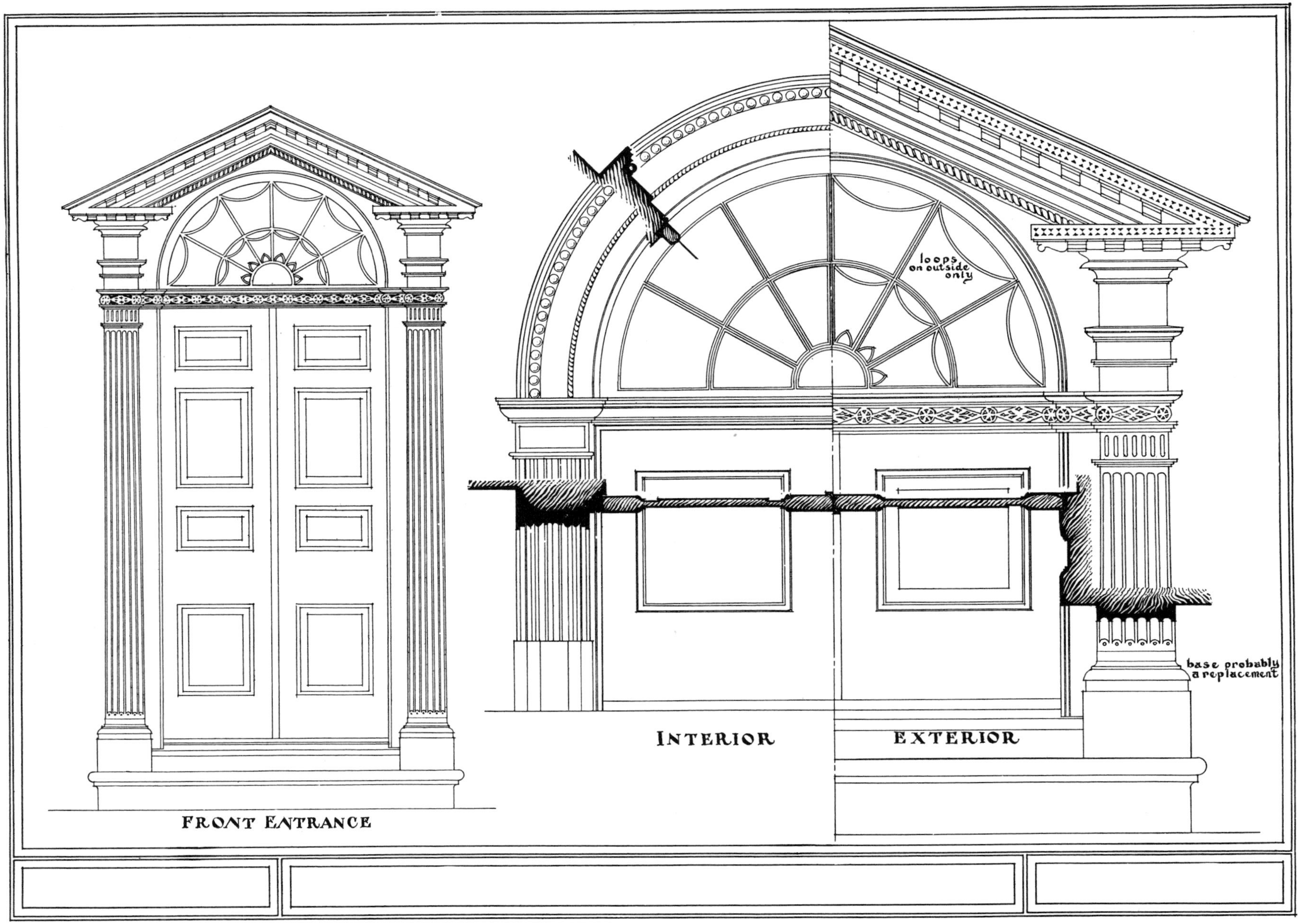

loops
on outside
only

base probably
a replacement

INTERIOR

EXTERIOR

FRONT ENTRANCE

THE MAGWOOD HOUSE

SCALE—ELEVATION—$\frac{13''}{32} = 1'-0''$.   DETAIL—$\frac{13''}{16} = 1'-0''$

THE HEYWARD HOUSE. 31 LEGARÉ STREET

THE HEYWARD HOUSE

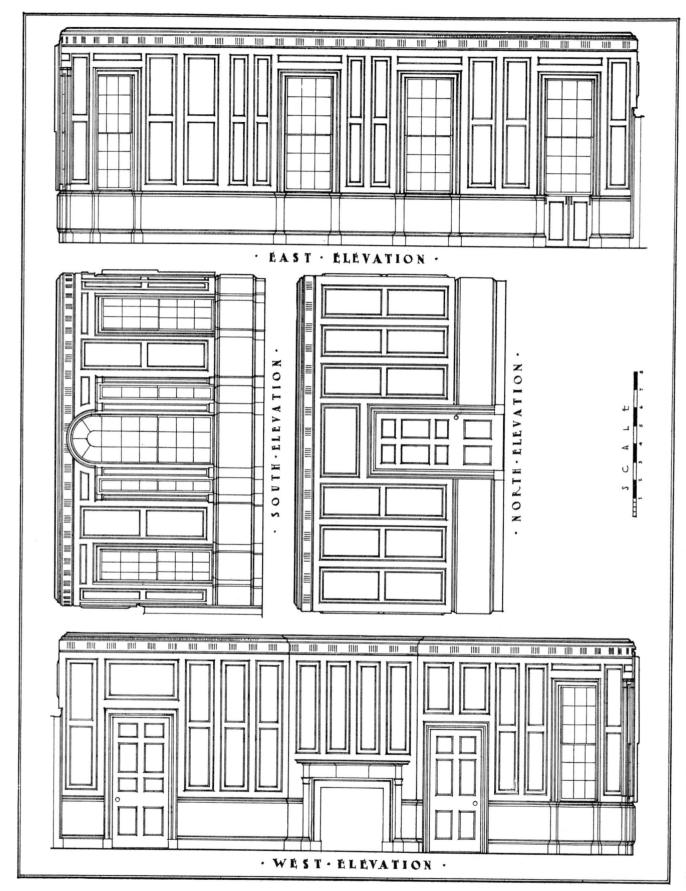

· EAST · ELEVATION ·

· SOUTH · ELEVATION ·

· NORTH · ELEVATION ·

· WEST · ELEVATION ·

DRAWN BY ALBERT GRAESER

THE HEYWARD HOUSE—DRAWING-ROOM

SCALE
1 2 3 4 5 6 7 8

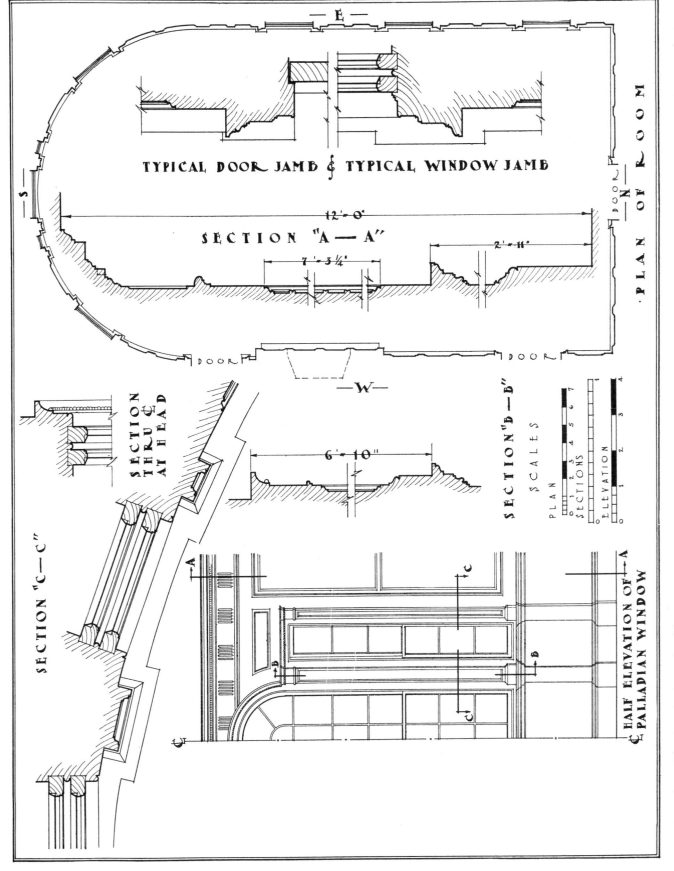

TYPICAL DOOR JAMB & TYPICAL WINDOW JAMB

SECTION "A — A"

12'-0'

7'-3¼'

2'-11'

SECTION "B—B"

6'-10"

SCALES

PLAN

SECTIONS
0 1 2 3 4 5 6 7

ELEVATION
0 1 2 3 4

SECTION "C—C"

SECTION THRU ℄ AT HEAD

℄ HALF ELEVATION OF PALLADIAN WINDOW

· PLAN OF ROOM ·

DOOR

DOOR

DOOR

—E—

—S—

—N—

—W—

DRAWN BY ALBERT GRAESER

THE HEYWARD HOUSE—DRAWING-ROOM

168

DOCTOR ANDREW TURNBULL'S SHOP—1780. NOW IN THE CHARLESTON MUSEUM

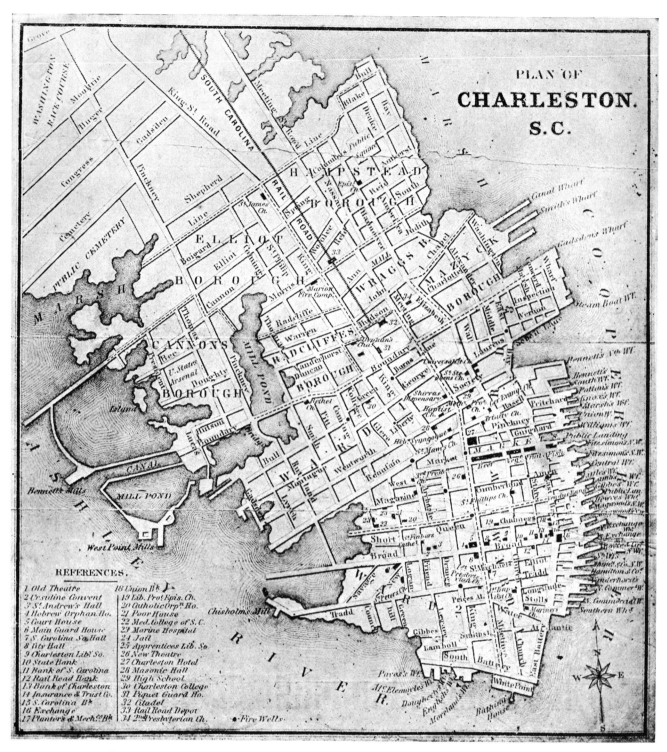

REFERENCES.

1 Old Theatre
2 Ursuline Convent
3 St. Andrew's Hall
4 Hebrew Orphan Ho.
5 Court House
6 Main Guard House
7 S. Carolina So. Hall
8 City Hall
9 Charleston Lib? So.
10 State Bank
11 Bank of S. Carolina
12 Rail Road Bank
13 Bank of Charleston
14 Insurance & Trust Co.
15 S. Carolina Bk
16 Exchange
17 Planters & Mech.Co.Bk

18 Union Bk
19 Lib. Prot.Epis. Ch.
20 Catholic Orpn Ho.
21 Poor House
22 Med.College of S.C.
23 Marine Hospital
24 Jail
25 Apprentices Lib. So
26 New Theatre
27 Charleston Hotel
28 Masonic Hall
29 High School
30 Charleston College
31 Piquet Guard Ho.
32 Citadel
33 Rail Road Depot
34 2nd Presbyterian Ch.

• Fire Wells

CHARLESTON— 1849

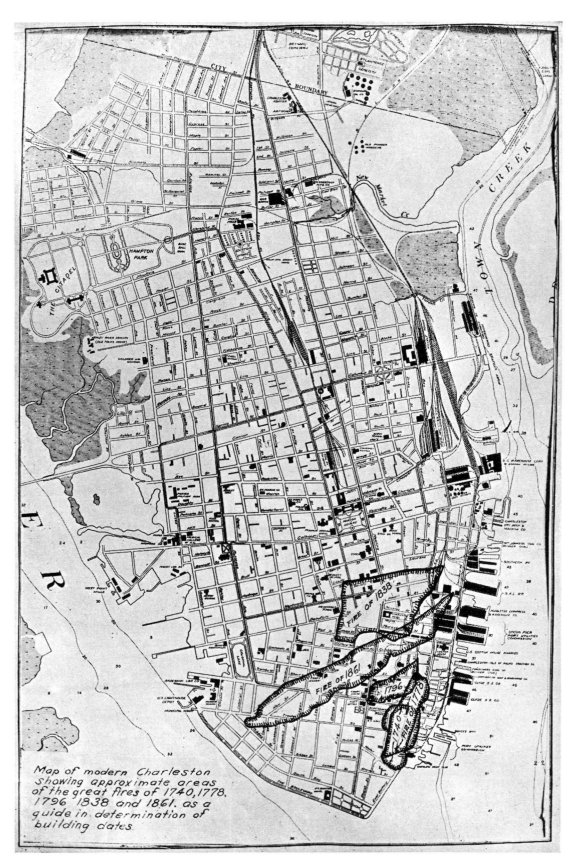

Map of modern Charleston showing approximate areas of the great fires of 1740, 1778, 1796 1838 and 1861. as a guide in determination of building dates.

CHARLESTON—THE FIRE AREAS, DRAWN IN 1925

THE ANTE-BELLUM PERIOD

ETWEEN the post-Revolutionary and the ante-bellum periods lies the decade 1815–25, which might be considered as an era of transition. During these years the country as a whole turned its attention from foreign problems and dangers to more intensive development of its own resources.

Prior to the invention of Eli Whitney's cotton gin, in 1793, only long-stapled cotton grown on the sea islands had proved a profitable crop, owing to the difficulty of separating the seed from short-staple by hand. With this new mechanical aid, the short-staple cotton, grown inland, could be made lucrative, thus leading to the enormous advance in cotton acreage, attended by the increasing use of slave labor, which, before 1810, had been on the decline throughout the country. Before 1834, however, South Carolina had begun to fall behind in the quantity of cotton produced, owing to the exhaustion of the soil under the system of cultivation then in use, and it was found that slave labor could be used only to the best advantage in developing new land; and slavery was becoming less and less profitable, and it seemed likely it would have gone out when the economic necessity no longer existed.

In the early part of the century most of the states had spent considerable sums on canals as a means of inland transportation. The second in the country was the Santee Canal, twenty miles long, connecting the Santee and Cooper rivers, which was completed in 1800. Canals were later to be supplanted by railroads, and the first train in the United States ran from Charleston to Hamburg, on the Savannah River, opposite Augusta. The South Carolina Railroad was accomplished from Charleston to Columbia, and later to Camden, by 1850.

The improved textile machinery first used in England, then in France, and finally in New England, created an ever-growing demand for raw cotton, and precluded the diversification of crops or the development of other resources to any great extent in the South. In 1817, the first rice mill operated by steam was built in Charleston. Despite the rising tide of industrialism throughout the North, the South clung to agriculture, and found her interests and growth isolated from the rest of the country as a whole. The decade of the forties was one of extraordinary prosperity and continued on into the fifties.

As the traditions of the post-Revolutionary period disappear, the craftsman-builder and his work count for less and less, and the architect and his activities emerge into prominence. We hear of James Hoban, a medal-man from the Dublin Society of Arts, coming to South Carolina, and, through Colonel Laurens, gaining the official patronage of Washington. The first thoroughly trained Charleston-born architect was Robert Mills, deriving his professional background from both Latrobe and Jefferson. His buildings in his native city are now limited to the First Baptist Church and the County Records Building, the latter being, it is said, the first all-fireproof construction attempted in this country. He also prepared plans for the enlargement of St. Michael's Church, in his characteristically austere manner; happily these were never executed. Besides architecture, Mills devoted much time to practical problems of civil engineering and surveying, and his atlas of South Carolina is probably the most comprehensive ever made of the state. As much of his most distinguished work was executed in Richmond, Baltimore, and Washington, it need not be touched on here.

In 1826, the Board of Trustees of the College of Charleston (founded in 1770) "apply to Mr. Strickland," of Philadelphia, for a plan for a college building. In 1846, this structure was amplified by the addition of a portico and lateral wings, added by Colonel E. Brickell White, a Charlestonian, and a graduate of West Point. He was in residence in the city at that time, supervising the erection of the new Federal Custom House, and along with this official duty carried on an extensive practice. Later he served as a colonel of artillery in the Confederate Army, and continued to practice after the war. His most distinctive creation, however, is the spire of St. Philip's, which he added to the church and tower by Joseph Hyde when the building was reërected after the fire of 1835. In the Huguenot Church and in Grace Episcopal Church (1848), Colonel White departs from the classic tradition and essays his skill in the manner of the Gothic Revival. Before this time, stables and coach-houses had been built with pointed windows and crenellated gables, but their builders had evidently created these anachronisms in a spirit of pleasantry, and had not regarded them seriously. But with the rise of the romantic movement, architects displayed their erudition by producing buildings in different styles for different purposes. This was a fallacy into which the older generation of craftsmen-builders had never been led, and was a distinctive loss to the harmonious character which the town must have possessed up to this time.

Colonel White's most active competitor was the firm of Jones & Lee, evidently younger men. In the Unitarian Church, they score on Colonel White by reproducing, in lath and plaster, the fan-vaulting of Henry VII's Chapel. In St. Luke's Episcopal Church their work was interrupted by the war. Lee served as captain of engineers and assisted General Beauregard in his fight against the Federal blockade by the ingenious invention of a spar-torpedo. After the war, while still a comparatively young man, he emigrated to St. Louis, where he resumed the practice of architecture with renewed success. Besides these leading practitioners there were a number of lesser as well as out-of-town men who did occasional work.

Shortly after the close of the Revolution, Jonathan Lucas, an English mill-wright, was shipwrecked near the mouth of the Santee River. Here he erected, in 1817, the first waterpower rice mill, and soon created an extensive business throughout the Tidewater Country, which continued to be carried on by three generations of the same name. There were numerous rice mills built in Charleston, three of which have survived to the present day—Chisolm's Mill, Bennett's Mill, and West Point Rice Mills. They show that in this period the design of commercial buildings was given as much consideration as that of public buildings or dwellings. Essentially factories, their proportions, the proper relationship of voids and solids, and the light-and-shade effects of surfaces were all carefully studied, and conformed admirably with the architecture of the city. Far from being eye-sores, they were imposing monuments, and in Bennett's Mil may be seen the height of a distinctly Palladian version of industrial architecture.1

Many of the buildings that we have considered owe a great deal of their character and distinction to the presence of wrought-iron gates, fences, balconies, and grilles. Much of this iron-work was made during ante-bellum times (i. e., prior to 1861), or even later, for the traditions of this craft have survived to the present day.

The earliest iron-worker we know of was Tunis Tebaut; he, and a partner, William Johnson, were recorded before the Revolution as "blacksmiths," carrying on an extensive business on "Beal's Wharf." At an earlier date, the name Tebaut appears among the Huguenot settlers on the Santee. Works attributed to him by tradition are several fences and gates around churches erected in post-Revolutionary times.

In 1820, Iusti came to Charleston from Germany. His best-known works are the gates of St. Michael's Church Yard, which bear the inscription "Iusti Fecit."

Werner came over from Germany in 1828, and as late as 1870 was still working. He ran an extensive business, with numerous helpers, including among others a white man named Dothage, and "Uncle Toby Richardson," colored. Many of Werner's pieces are repetitions of the same few designs. This may be accounted for by the execution having been delegated to assistants, and to the fact that he was burnt out and lost all of his patterns. He is responsible for much cast iron, similar in design to that in many other cities of this period.

In 1847, the last German iron-worker, Frederic Julius Ortmann, came here from Baden-Baden. He had hardly established himself when the war came on and he served with the local German militia in the defense of his adopted city. After the war he resumed his craft, which is continued to this day by his sons, following the precedents established by Werner almost a century ago.

Of the ante-bellum dwelling-houses, the most striking characteristic is the tendency toward the grandiose and magnificent, tempered by an almost academic classicism. This is exemplified in the use of porticos of the colossal order, usually derived from the monument of Lysikrates or from the Tower of the Winds, so enticingly illustrated in the "Antiquities of Athens." Ceilings attain an unprecedented loftiness, with tall, narrow windows extending to the floor, giving access to balconies, or protected by cast-iron grilles of anthemion patterns. The wainscot disappears, leaving as its survival a very high baseboard of massive mouldings. Mantels lose entirely their genial cheerfulness and become truncated Greek doorways executed in black-and-gold-veined marble. To accomplish the altitude of the second story, the stair winds up in a great hemicycle at the end of a hall with, somewhere along its flight, a niche sheltering a marble Amazon or a bronze of Lord Byron. The furniture was mostly of Empire design, with a good deal of brass mounting. Tall French mirrors, set over mantels or between windows, enhanced the apparent size of the apartments and reflected the glow of crimson damask hangings and the quiet hues of Sully portraits. It was essentially an age of dominant and forceful individuals, who, in the character of their homes, expressed their personalities without reserve. Most of what was then admired is dismissed today with the general condemnation of being "early Victorian," without being given the benefit of unprejudiced critical judgment.

In the foregoing we have attempted briefly to point out something of the sequence in the physical development of the town; to stress those fleeting periods when, under favorable economic conditions, wealth accumulated and expressed its ideals and tastes in enduring fabrics, even as affluence faded into poverty to reappear again in newer modes and enthusiasms.

ALBERT SIMONS, A. I. A.
SAMUEL LAPHAM, JR., A. I. A.

ST. PHILIP'S CHURCH—THE STEEPLE, E. BRICKELL WHITE, ARCHITECT

ST. PHILIP'S CHURCH — 1835. JOSEPH HYDE, ARCHITECT

ST. PHILIP'S CHURCH—CHOIR AND CHANCEL—1920. SIMONS AND LAPHAM, ARCHITECTS

180

ST. PHILIP'S CHURCH — PARISH HOUSE

ST. PHILIP'S CHURCH

CONGREGATIONAL CHURCH — PARISH HOUSE

UNITARIAN CHURCH (FOREGROUND) — 1852

EDWARD C. JONES AND FRANCIS D. LEE, ARCHITECTS

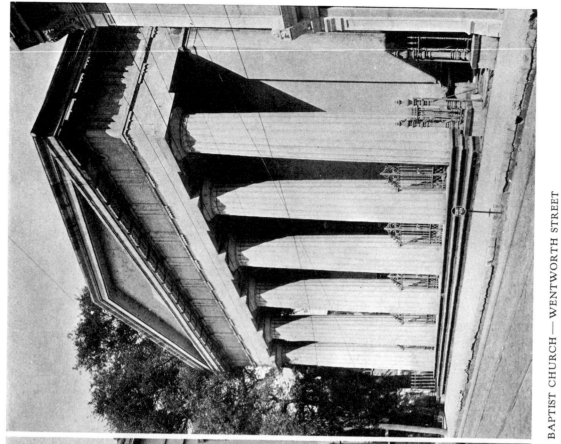

BAPTIST CHURCH — WENTWORTH STREET

SYNAGOGUE — HAZEL STREET — 1838
— WARNER (NEW YORK), ARCHITECT

THE HUGUENOT CHURCH—1844. E. BRICKELL WHITE, ARCHITECT

FIRST BAPTIST CHURCH — 1822.   ROBERT MILLS, ARCHITECT

MESNE CONVEYANCE OFFICE—"FIREPROOF BUILDING"—1822. ROBERT MILLS, ARCHITECT

WESTMINSTER PRESBYTERIAN CHURCH — 1850 (TOP). EDWARD C. JONES, ARCHITECT
BETHEL METHODIST CHURCH — 1853 (BOTTOM)

MERCHANTS' OFFICES. 1 PRIOLEAU STREET

COLLEGE OF CHARLESTON—CENTRAL PORTION, WILLIAM STRICKLAND, ARCHITECT—1828.
WINGS AND PORTICO, E. BRICKELL WHITE, ARCHITECT—1850. GATE LODGE, BEFORE 1852,
E. BRICKELL WHITE, ARCHITECT (PROBABLY)

MARKET HALL—1841. E. BRICKELL WHITE, ARCHITECT

GATE—CITY HALL PARK

GATE—HIBERNIAN HALL—1840

ST. MICHAEL'S CHURCH GATE—1840. IUSTI, MAKER

McLEISH'S SMITHY. 4 CUMBERLAND STREET

THE CITADEL — 1829–32.   FREDERICK WESNER, ARCHITECT

CHARLESTON HOTEL — BEFORE 1857.   —— REICHARDT, ARCHITECT

REAR GATE

PLANTERS AND MECHANICS BANK, EAST BAY, BEFORE 1849.

PLANTERS AND MECHANICS BANK—SERVANTS' QUARTERS (TOP)
PLANTERS HOTEL (BOTTOM), BEFORE 1835. 137 CHURCH STREET

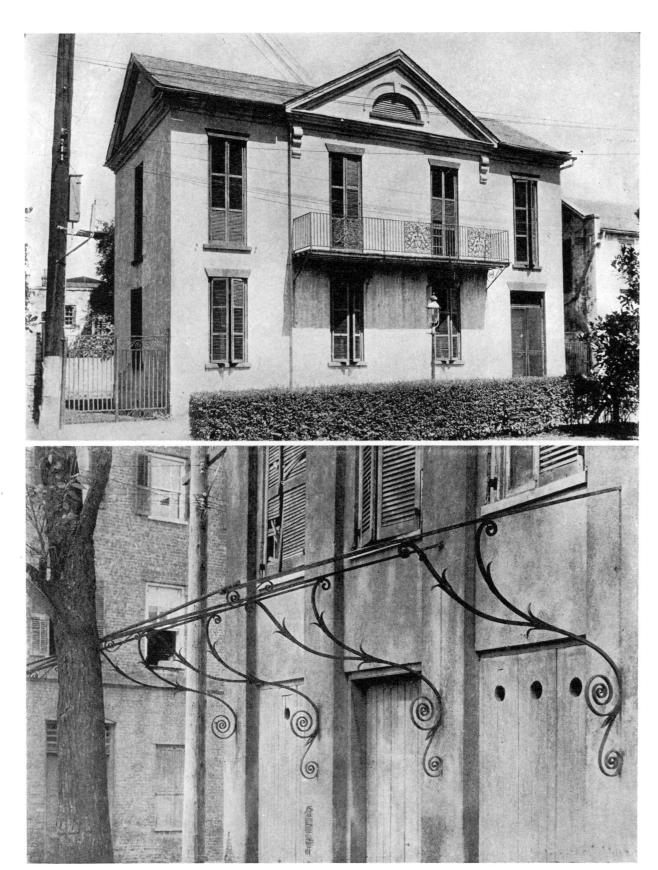

LAW-OFFICE OF JAMES LOUIS PETIGRU — 1848. ST. MICHAEL'S ALLEY (TOP). E. BRICKELL WHITE, ARCHITECT
WROUGHT-IRON AWNING SUPPORTS. 152 CHURCH STREET (BOTTOM)

BENNETT'S RICE MILL — 1844

CHISOLM'S RICE MILL — 1830 (TOP). WEST POINT RICE MILL — 1860 (BOTTOM)

HOUSE AT THE CORNER OF ANN AND MEETING STREETS

WILLIAM RAVENEL'S HOUSE—ABOUT 1845. 13 EAST BATTERY STREET. WILLIAM MASON SMITH'S HOUSE—1820. 26 MEETING STREET

ELIAS VANDERHORST'S HOUSE—AFTER 1832. 28 CHAPEL STREET

ELIAS VANDERHORST'S HOUSE (TOP)
CHARLES ALSTON'S HOUSE—1838. 21 EAST BATTERY (BOTTOM)

CHARLES ALSTON'S HOUSE

AIKEN ROW, WRAGG SQUARE

ROBERT MARTIN'S HOUSE—1834-1840. 16 CHARLOTTE STREET

ROBERT MARTIN'S HOUSE

HOUSE AT 75 ANSON STREET

THE RIPLEY HOUSE. 21 GEORGE STREET

JAMES NICHOLSON'S HOUSE—AFTER 1830. 172 RUTLEDGE AVENUE

JOSEPH AIKEN'S HOUSE—1848. 20 CHARLOTTE STREET

HOUSE AT 75 ASHLEY AVENUE

JAMES NICHOLSON'S HOUSE

WILLIAM ROPER'S HOUSE — AFTER 1845. 9 EAST BATTERY

THE SIMONTON GATE. 32 LEGARÉ STREET

THE SIMONTON GATE

SIGNATURES AND IDENTIFIED WORKS OF SOME OF THE EARLY ARCHITECTS AND BUILDERS OF CHARLESTON

⚭

PETER HORLBECK
For signature see page 217
Born —— *Died* ——

JOHN HORLBECK
For signature see page 217
Born 1729. Died ——

PRACTICED AS

PETER AND JOHN HORLBECK
Circa 1767 - 1792

IDENTIFIED BUILDINGS:
The Exchange, 1767, Builders
The Exchange was designed by WILLIAM RIGBY NAYLOR in 1766
The Synagogue, 1792 (Steedman & Horlbeck). Destroyed 1838

GABRIEL MANIGAULT

Born 1758. Died 1809

IDENTIFIED BUILDINGS:
Joseph Manigault House, Meeting and John Sts.
About 1790
Gabriel Manigault House, Meeting and George Sts.
About 1800
Bank of the United States, 1801
Chapel of the Orphan House, 1802
South Carolina Society Hall, 1804

WILLIAM STRICKLAND
OF PHILADELPHIA

IDENTIFIED BUILDING:
Main Building, College of Charleston, 1828

JOSEPH HYDE
Born —— *Died* ——
Practiced circa 1835 - 1840

IDENTIFIED BUILDINGS:
St. Philip's Church, 1835
Masonic Temple, Market St. Destroyed 1838
Market Hall (?), 1841

ROBERT MILLS
For signature see page 217
Born 1781. Died 1855

IDENTIFIED BUILDINGS:
First Baptist Church, 1822
County Record Building, 1822
Circular Church, 1804. Destroyed 1861

—— WARNER
OF NEW YORK
Synagogue, Beth Elohim, 1838

FREDERICK WESNER
Born —— *Died* ——
Practiced circa 1813 - 1841

IDENTIFIED BUILDINGS:
Portico, South Carolina Society Hall, 1825
The Citadel, 1829-32
Old Medical College, 1827

EDWARD BRICKELL WHITE

Born 1806   Died 1882
Practiced circa 1841-1876

IDENTIFIED BUILDINGS:

Huguenot Church, 1844
Grace Church, 1848
Petigru Law Office, 1848
College of Charleston, Wings of Main Building, 1850
U. S. Custom House, 1850
Spire of St. Philip's Church
Charleston Gas Light Co. Office, 141 Meeting St., 1876

G. C. WALKER

College of Charleston, Library Building, 1855

FRANCIS D. LEE

EDWARD C. JONES

Born —— Died ——

Born 1826.   Died 1885
Removed from Charleston to St. Louis, Mo., in 1868

PRACTICED INDIVIDUALLY AND AS FIRM OF

JONES AND LEE
Circa 1849-1862

IDENTIFIED BUILDINGS:

Westminster Presbyterian Church, 1850 (Edward C. Jones)
Unitarian Church, 1852 (Jones and Lee)
State Bank of South Carolina, No. 1 Broad St., 1853 (Francis D. Lee)
Farmers and Exchange Bank, 135 East Bay, 1854 (Jones and Lee)
Remodeling of Charleston Orphan House, 1855 (Jones and Lee)
Citadel Square Baptist Church, 1856 (Jones and Lee)
St. Luke's Episcopal Church, 1862 (Francis D. Lee)

be paid to the Bill of Particulars preceeding this, when you contract with the Bricklayer relative to the Use of Stone Lime instead of Shell Lime; The Superiority of the first above the last always gives it the Preeminence; but particularly so, in the Conjunction of new & Old Work.

I have calculated on the different Pieces of Work, the highest Prices and if my measurements have been as correct, as have been my Desire and Attention to have them so, I will not hesitate in saying that the fund requisite to compleat this Addition shall not exceed Dlls 10,000 which will be less than One half of what the obtained Pews will bring, estimating $400 Each for the Lower Pews & $250 Each for those in the Gallery.

Charleston South Carolina March 1804.

Robert Mills

Architect

Additional Pews below

execution and Administrators do Consent, Promise and Grant to and with the said Peter Mani...

Thomas Lynch, Henry Laurens, Benjamin D... Miles Brewton, John Rutledge and Charles Pinckney and th... Successors, for and on the behalf of the Public of ... Province by these presents in manner and Form following (...

Horlbeck their Heirs, Executors and Administrat... ...ne of them for the Consideration herein after mentioned shall a... in the Year of our Lord One thousand seven Hu... ...e and Seventy one, make, Erect and Build and set up in a Y... Ground AN EXCHANGE of the form, Dime... ...s and Materials herein after mentioned (that is to say)

Bricks and Mortar Ninety two feet from North ... ...uth, and Sixty five and one half feet from East to West; to b... shall be found, and to be Pilled and Planked ... ...n a manner ... the Commissioners or a Majority of... below the Surface of Broad Street and five feet six Inch... ...from the Surface of the Street to the inside Crown of the Arch... Inches from the Surface of Broad Street which Floor thr... ...ghout the whole to be supported with Nine Inch Groins m... The Wall of the North, South and West side of the said Building to be Four Bricks lengthways thick, And the Wa... thick from the Foundation to the Pincipal Floor The Cellars to divide into Six Apartments and Raised with good Bric...

Ja Parsons   Benjamin Dart   Henry Laurens   Ralph ...

John Horlbeck   Peter Horlbeck   C. Pinckney

ROBERT MILLS' SIGNATURE TO THE PROPOSAL FOR ENLARGING ST. MICHAEL'S (TOP)
JOHN AND PETER HORLBECK'S SIGNATURES TO THE CONTRACT FOR BUILDING THE EXCHANGE (BOTTOM)

BIBLIOGRAPHY

BAIRD, C. W.: History of the Huguenot Emigration to America. 1885.

BAPTIST CHURCH, CHARLESTON, HISTORY OF.

BRACKETT, G. R.: History of the Second Presbyterian Church. 1898.

BROWN, E. C. L.: Sketch of the Unitarian Church, Charleston. 1882.

CITY OF CHARLESTON, YEAR BOOKS, 1880–1890.

CITY OF CHARLESTON DIRECTORIES, 1790–1852.

CITY GAZETTE AND DAILY COMMERCIAL ADVERTISER, 1788–1832.

CLARK, W. A.: Banking Institutions in South Carolina prior to 1860. 1922.

COLLEGE OF CHARLESTON: Trustees' Minutes, 1790–1880.

COMMONS JOURNAL MS. AND COUNCIL JOURNAL MS.

COURIER, THE CHARLESTON, 1803–1860.

DALCHO, FREDERICK: Church History of South Carolina. 1820.

FRAZIER, CHARLES: Reminiscences of Charleston. 1854.

                Corner Stone Address, College of Charleston. 1828.

GILMAN, SAMUEL: The Old and the New (Unitarian Church). 1854.

HARLOW, R. V.: The Growth of the United States.

HOLMES, G. S.: Historical Sketch of St. Michael's Church. 1887.

HOPKINS, T. F.: Historical Sketch of St. Mary's Church. 1897.

HORN, E. T.: Historical Sketch of St. John's Lutheran Church. 1884.

HOWE, GEORGE: History of the Presbyterian Church in South Carolina. 1870.

HUGUENOT CHURCH, SKETCH OF. 1885.

HUGUENOT SOCIETY OF SOUTH CAROLINA, TRANSACTIONS OF.

LAPHAM, SAMUEL, JR.: The Rice Mills of Charleston, S. C. (Architectural Record, August, 1923).

LEVIN, NATHANIEL: Synagogue Beth Elohim. 1883.

McCRADY, EDWARD: South Carolina under Proprietary Government. 1897.

                South Carolina under Royal Government. 1899.

                Historical Sketch, St. Philip's Church. 1896.

                Address Medical College Commencement. 1886.

MESNE CONVEYANCE OFFICE: Deeds and Records.

MISSILDINE, A. H.: Historical Sketch of Congregational Church. 1882.

POYAS, MRS. (THE ANCIENT LADY): Our Forefathers, Their Homes and Their Churches.

PRESBYTERIAN CENTENNIAL. 1914.

RAMSEY, DAVID: History of South Carolina. 1809.

RAVENEL, BEATRICE ST. JULIEN: Architects of Charleston (Carolina Art Association, 1945).

RIVERS, W. J.: Historical Sketch of South Carolina. 1856.

SIMONS, ALBERT: Minor Charleston Houses (The Architectural Forum, February, 1925).

SIMONS, ALBERT, AND LAPHAM, S., JR.: The Development of Charleston Architecture (The Architectural Forum, October, 1923, to January, 1924).

                Early Iron Work in Charleston (The Architectural Forum, April, 1926).

SMITH, A. R. HUGER AND D. E. HUGER: The Dwelling Houses of Charleston. 1917.

SMYTHE, A. T.: History of the Hibernian Society. 1901.

SOUTH CAROLINA GAZETTE, THE, 1732–1801.

SOUTH CAROLINA HISTORICAL AND GENEALOGICAL MAGAZINE.

WILSON, C. C.: Robert Mills, Bulletin of the University of South Carolina, No. 77. 1919.

WALLACE, D. D.: Life of Henry Laurens.

INDEX

Text Type: Kennerly Old Style
Text: Finch Fine VHF
80# white
Cover: Curtis Gradations
80# *Plum Haze*